THE RISE OF LIFE
THE FIRST 3·5 BILLION YEARS

THE RISE OF LIFE
THE FIRST 3·5 BILLION YEARS

John Reader
Illustrations by John Gurche

ALFRED A. KNOPF
NEW YORK
1986

THIS IS A BORZOI BOOK
PUBLISHED BY ALFRED A. KNOPF, INC.

First American Edition

This book was created and produced by Roxby Prehistory Limited
a division of Roxby Press
98 Clapham Common North Side
London SW4 9SG

Editor: Gilly Abrahams
Design: Eric Drewery
Typesetting: Tradespools Limited, Frome, Somerset
Reproduction: F.E. Burman Limited

Library of Congress Cataloging-in-Publication Data

Reader, John.
The rise of life.
Includes index.
I. Title.
QH325.R395 1986   560   86–7316
ISBN 0–394–74051–3 (pbk.)

Printed and bound in Spain by
TONSA, San Sebastian

The text of this book was written during the summer of Alice's sixth year. Her company, and her quizzical interest in the things I was writing about, were often an inspiration and I hope she may one day regard this book as a token of the happy times we spent together.

John Reader

I would like to thank the person to whom I am indebted more than any other. For her enthusiasm, sacrifice and intelligent contributions, I thank Ms Carolyn Gamble.

John Gurche

CONTENTS

INTRODUCTION
9

'What I'm really interested in is whether God could have made the world in a different way; that is, whether the necessity of logical simplicity leaves any freedom at all.'

Albert Einstein

INTRODUCTION

The story of life on Earth begins with a multitude of very simple organisms swarming through the warm seas that covered a good deal of the Earth's surface nearly four billion years ago. Organisms so tiny that 100,000 of them might comfortably occupy the space within this O; each a single independent living thing, a cell, made of chemical substances, sustaining itself on chemical substances absorbed direct from the water and reproducing itself by enlarging a little then splitting into two. Where there was one there were now two identical cells, then four, eight, sixteen.... These simple organisms were the basic units from which all forms of life have evolved – bacteria, plants, fish, reptiles, mammals and man, everything. The essential ingredients and processes of life were already present in every one of them. Through time, chance and changing environmental circumstance directed the modifications that have produced today's living world.

Once life began, its story becomes a logical, not to say inevitable sequence of evolutionary cause and effect, which science is able to recount in fascinating detail, but just *how* life began is still something of a mystery, not incontrovertibly explained. The chemical constituents of living organisms have been identified, the biochemical processes that keep organisms alive are known in complex detail, but the vital spark that initiates life awaits precise definition. Life: so obvious and simple a phenomenon, yet so hard to explain.

The simplest explanation attributes life on Earth to the work of some supernatural force which has ordered that things should be so. This explanation has the unquestioned merit of encompassing everything; there is nothing that the invocation of a supernatural force cannot explain. No question remains if God was behind it all – belief in the existence of an omnipotent God is all that is required.

Down the ages such belief has provided comforting explanations of all life's mysteries, but as science discovered logical simplicity at work in so many natural phenomena and thereby explained the mysteries of night and day, the seasons, the movements of the stars, and so forth, the supernatural explanation of life on Earth seemed increasingly inadequate. The origin of life should be susceptible to simple, logical explanation, just like everything else.

If the supernatural is dismissed, then just two possible explanations remain: either life developed from the material constituents of the Earth by some process that should be understandable in terms of the chemical and physical laws that provide logical explanations of the rest of the Earth's characteristics; or else life originated in some other part of the universe and the Earth was, as it were, sown with the seeds of life from space.

The extraterrestrial explanation of life on Earth has a persuasive logic of numbers in its favour. The Earth is a planet circling a star – the Sun. The Sun is just one of perhaps 100 billion suns in our galaxy. Our galaxy is one of at least ten billion galaxies in the universe. Confronted with numbers of this order, some logical minds find it highly improbable that life could have arisen on Earth alone. Among all the countless galaxies and solar systems there must be many other planets on which conditions conducive to life exist, or have existed, they reason.

The Nobel prize-winning Italian physicist, Enrico Fermi, who, along with the Hungarian Leo Szilard, built the world's first atomic reactor in a Chicago squash court during World War II, once made a point of this numerical logic in a lecture. Life must have existed on other planets somewhere in the universe, he declared, other conscious beings must have evolved, other civilizations and technology must have developed and some highly intelligent beings must have conquered space. Surely they would not have overlooked the Earth in their travels? 'They should have arrived here by now,' Fermi concluded, 'so where are they?' His friend Leo Szilard quietly answered: 'They are among us, but they call themselves Hungarians.'

Though graced by humour and numerical logic, Fermi's proposal that life arrived on Earth in a fully-fledged form does nothing to explain the precise manner of its origin. A little closer to the point was the theory proposed by the Swedish physicist Svante Arrhenius in 1884.

Under the title *Panspermia* (meaning 'seeds everywhere' and first used by the Greek philosopher Anaxagoras in the fifth century BC to describe the doctrine of eternal life, wherein all new life arose from seeds which were everywhere and always present), Arrhenius showed that planetary air currents and volcanic eruptions could blast small particles, including micro-organisms, into space, whence they might travel between the stars and spread life through the universe. Arrhenius presented some very convincing calculations with his theory, showing that the micro-organisms would be propelled through space by the pressure of the Sun's rays and would travel beyond our solar system in 14 months; they could reach the nearest star in 9,000 years. Life might have come to Earth in the same manner, he proposed.

One major drawback to Arrhenius's panspermia theory, however, is the problem of explaining how organisms could have survived the lethal effects of radiation on their long journey through space, although this has not discouraged those to whom the panspermia idea appeals; indeed, it has challenged their imaginative ingenuity, even in modern times. In 1981, for instance, the biologist Francis Crick, another Nobel prize winner, nailed his colours to the panspermia mast with a suggestion that to avoid damage the micro-organisms had travelled in the head of an unmanned spaceship, sent to Earth by a higher civilization which had developed elsewhere in the universe billions of years ago. Crick called this solution Directed Panspermia.

Another variation on the panspermia theme has come from the British astronomer Sir Fred Hoyle, who suggests that living micro-

Sir Fred Hoyle, the noted British astronomer, claims that evidence gathered from Halley's comet in 1986 will confirm his belief that life came to our planet from outer space.

TIME CHART

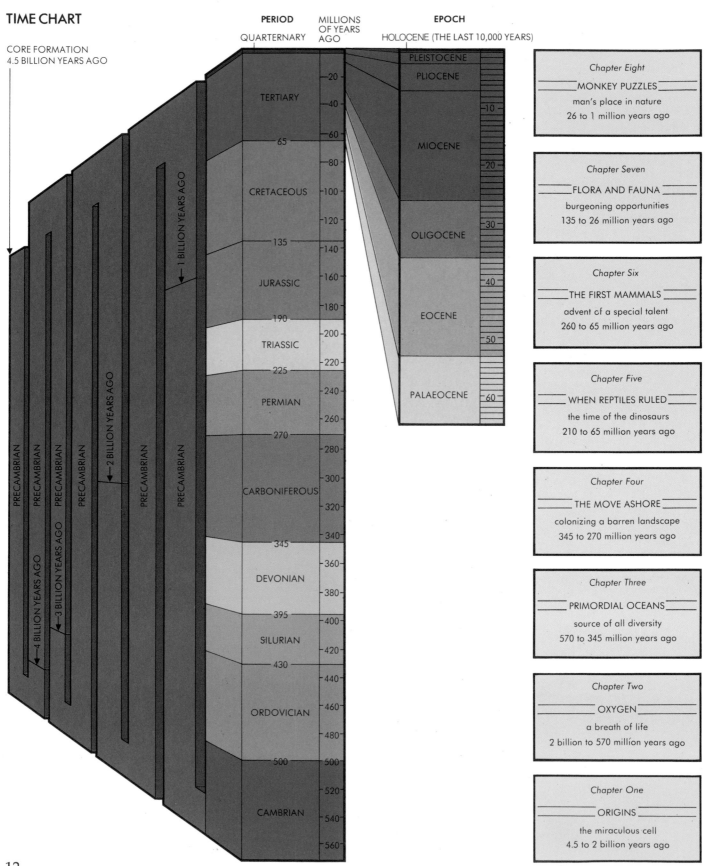

CORE FORMATION
4.5 BILLION YEARS AGO

PERIOD

MILLIONS OF YEARS AGO

EPOCH

QUARTERNARY

HOLOCENE (THE LAST 10,000 YEARS)

PLEISTOCENE

PLIOCENE

TERTIARY

-20

-40

-60

-10

MIOCENE

-20

-65

-80

CRETACEOUS

-100

-120

OLIGOCENE

-30

-135

-140

-160

EOCENE

-40

JURASSIC

-180

-190

-200

-50

TRIASSIC

-220

-225

PALAEOCENE

-60

PERMIAN

-240

-260

-270

-280

-300

CARBONIFEROUS

-320

-340

-345

-360

DEVONIAN

-380

-395

-400

SILURIAN

-420

-430

-440

-460

ORDOVICIAN

-480

-500

-500

-520

CAMBRIAN

-540

-560

PRECAMBRIAN

1 BILLION YEARS AGO

2 BILLION YEARS AGO

3 BILLION YEARS AGO

4 BILLION YEARS AGO

Chapter Eight

_____MONKEY PUZZLES_____

man's place in nature
26 to 1 million years ago

Chapter Seven

_____FLORA AND FAUNA_____

burgeoning opportunities
135 to 26 million years ago

Chapter Six

_____THE FIRST MAMMALS_____

advent of a special talent
260 to 65 million years ago

Chapter Five

_____WHEN REPTILES RULED_____

the time of the dinosaurs
210 to 65 million years ago

Chapter Four

_____THE MOVE ASHORE_____

colonizing a barren landscape
345 to 270 million years ago

Chapter Three

_____PRIMORDIAL OCEANS_____

source of all diversity
570 to 345 million years ago

Chapter Two

_____OXYGEN_____

a breath of life
2 billion to 570 million years ago

Chapter One

_____ORIGINS_____

the miraculous cell
4.5 to 2 billion years ago

12

organisms are prevalent among the dust particles that astronomers have observed drifting among the stars. The micro-organisms are occasionally incorporated in the core of comets where, in a protected aqueous environment, they multiply prodigiously. Some of these comets have brought life to Earth, Hoyle contends.

Hoyle is probably the most dedicated modern advocate of the idea that life came to Earth from space. He has published a string of books and articles on the subject – both popular and academic. His reputation, combined with his down-to-earth bulk and Yorkshire manner, command respect for his proposals, and although many experts refute them vehemently, no one has yet disproved them and thereby ruled panspermia and Hoyle out of court.

But even so, Hoyle, Crick and the panspermia idea only address the question of where life originated. They go no way towards answering the more basic question of how life originated, so in the end it seems that the extraterrestrial explanation of life on Earth is no more satisfactory than the suggestion that a supernatural force had arranged it all. This leaves us with the proposal that life developed from the material constituents of the Earth by some logical process, and the rest of this book aims to present a contemporary view of that process: not a definitive last word on exactly what happened, more one man's attempt to draw from the relevant fields of current enquiry a logical sequence of cause and effect in the progression of life on Earth.

*　　*　　*

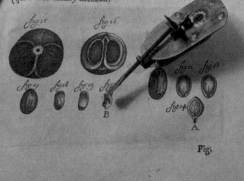

Chapter One

ORIGINS

the miraculous cell

A fantastic, vital world of infinite detail was revealed to the Dutch naturalist Anton van Leeuwenhoek in the late 17th century. Using simple, home-made microscopes (lower left), he described a multitude of hitherto unseen, unimaginably small objects. In 1665 Robert Hooke introduced the word 'cell' to natural science in a description of the structure of cork (centre); and in 1839 the German anatomist Theodor Schwann (top) showed that the cell is the basic component of all living things.

In the third century BC the Greek philosopher Aristotle applied much thought to the questions of life and how it might have originated. Indeed, his investigations in biology are probably among the most important ever undertaken, in terms of their influence, although this is often overshadowed by the attention given to his philosophical, ethical, political and physical works. Aristotle defined the economy of life – 'Nature does nothing to no purpose'; he described how the structure and behaviour of living things is related to the kind of environment they inhabit; he believed that animals developed from a nutritive substance contained in the female, which was given shape by semen. But he also said that life, in the first instance, is formed by the inherent energy of the primary elements – earth, water, air and fire – which moulds and organizes inert matter into living things.

This energy, which Aristotle called the 'entelechy' of living things, might also be described as the soul, the essence, the spirit of life. Aristotle believed it to be present in the elements to varying degrees, producing various organisms accordingly. Thus fireflies and many other insects were said to develop from the morning dew, while fleas, bedbugs and lice were generated in sand and the slime of wells, rivers and the sea. Crabs sprang from decaying slimes, eels and many kinds of fish from wet ooze and rotting seaweeds. Mice came initially from moist soil, so too did many of the higher animals, although man first appeared on Earth in the form of a worm. The process was called *generatio spontanea* – spontaneous generation.

Aristotle expounded his theories of life and its origins principally in his four works: *On the Origin of Animals, On the Movements of Animals, On the Parts of Animals* and *On Plants*. Subsequently, these works became the foundation of scientific culture; not surprisingly, therefore, the principle of spontaneous generation stood for a long time as the unquestioned explanation of the origin of life on Earth, with the exception of man, whose origin was satisfactorily explained in the Bible.

As the era of scientific experimentation dawned in the early seventeenth century, there were some notable instances of experiments conducted with a view to proving that spontaneous generation certainly did occur.

The Belgian chemist and physiologist Jan Baptist van Helmont (1577–1644), for example, was the first man to set up experiments capable of defining the nutrition of plants, but he is much more famous for a description of how to obtain live mice from wheat grains. He recorded how he put a dirty shirt in a tub of grain and 21 days later found it seething with live mice; van Helmont believed that human sweat was the generating essence at work in this case. Pursuing his experiment just a little further, he noted in all seriousness that these artificially produced mice were exact replicas of natural mice caught and bred in the house.

At that time science had yet to make the crucial distinction between experiments designed to test a theory and those designed to prove it. Van Helmont wanted to prove that spontaneous generation occurred, and did so to his satisfaction. A few years later the Tuscan physican Francesco Redi took the alternative approach and set up a series of experiments designed to test, rather than simply prove, the theory of spontaneous generation.

In a treatise published in 1668 Redi described how he placed meat in a series of large jars, some covered with muslin, others left open. Flies swarmed around all the jars, but little white worms appeared only in the meat that had been left uncovered. They came from the eggs that flies had deposited, he said, not spontaneously from bad meat as was previously believed, and he concluded that decaying matter merely offers a feeding place for hatching insects.

Another important point that must be borne in mind when considering the theory of spontaneous generation or, indeed, any early observation concerning life and its origin, is the limitation of the human eye. Even a man as perceptive as Aristotle could only see as much as the lens of his eye could resolve; nothing smaller existed. So when tiny growing organisms crossed the threshold of the eye's resolution, their arrival in the visible living world must indeed have seemed spontaneous.

The magnifying glass enlarged the dimensions of the living world to a small degree, and the microscope invented in 1590 by two Dutch opticians, Francis and Zachary Janssen, took the process just a stage further. But the Janssen instrument was a very crude affair, giving magnifications of only about ten times. Another Dutchman, Anton van Leeuwenhoek (1632–1723), was primarily responsible for the next major development. Leeuwenhoek built a series of simple but extremely effective instruments whose very short focal length lenses gave magnifications of up to 275 times and made possible the first extensive forays beyond the limits of the visible world.

At a time when the European powers were sending ships scouring the globe for new territory, wealth and wonder, Leeuwenhoek discovered an entire new world to explore without moving from his study in Delft. He described all he saw through his lenses in long letters that he addressed to the Royal Society in London. Full of quaint charm, these letters gave details of the living creatures that he found in rain, pond, river and sea water; in blood, semen, tooth scrapings and much else besides. Leeuwenhoek described red blood cells, and the manner in which blood circulates through the webbed foot of the frog, the ear of the rabbit and the tail of the eel. He observed the behaviour of human spermatozoa as 'they lashed their tails some eight or ten times in advancing a hair's breadth'. He watched fleas and weevils hatching from their minuscule eggs, and thus put paid to another tenet of spontaneous generation, since they clearly could no longer be said to spring ready made from sand and wheat dust. But most important of all, Leeuwenhoek took science appreciably closer to the recognition of life's basic form: the cell.

Robert Hooke (1635–1703) coined the term 'cell' in 1665, to describe the honeycomb pattern he had observed in thin slices of cork viewed through an early microscope. Hooke was actually referring to the spaces in the honeycomb as cells, like tiny rooms, not the material structure of the walls dividing them, and for the time being his definition and Leeuwenhoek's discovery of living microscopic organisms represented the limits of knowledge concerning the cellular basis of life. Not until nearly 150 years later, when the invention of achromatic lenses brought greater magnification and enhanced clarity to the microscope, was it recognized that the cell is in fact the common denominator of all living things.

In 1838 Matthias Schleiden described how all plants are composed of individual cells. Meanwhile, a German anatomist, Theodor Schwann, had found that cells were the basis of all animal tissue too. Aware of the work of Schleiden and others, Schwann drew the obvious conclusion and published his theory of cells in 1839. Cells are the basic unit of life, he declared. All living things from microbe to plant and man are composed of cells, and the differences between them are determined by the number of cells involved and the manner in which they are organized. Small organisms have fewer cells, organised in a relatively uncomplicated manner. Large organisms contain vast numbers of cells, organized in often staggering complexity.

The discovery that all living things, plants and animals alike, are composed of cells, was one of the great landmarks in mankind's exploration of the living world. Following the work of Schleiden and Schwann, the French scientist Louis Pasteur effectively set the cap on the theory of cells as the basis of all life in 1864, with an experiment demonstrating conclusively that all cells, even the smallest bacteria, are the product of other cells. Pasteur's experiments were the ultimate disproof of spontaneous generation and also, incidentally, the basis of the pasteurization process that subsequently became such an important aspect of public health.

The realization that the cell is the basis of life led inevitably to the conclusion that to explain the origin of life science now need only explain the origin of the cell. But this idea, simple enough in itself, turned out to be a far more difficult task than anyone could have known. The human body, for example, is made up of around ten trillion cells, and every one of them is a package of sheer wonder. Since the days of Pasteur, Schwann, Schleiden, Hooke and Leeuwenhoek, a host of researchers, aided by a stream of technical innovations, have probed deep into the workings of this infinitesimally small, self-sustaining, self-replicating biochemical machine that is the secret of life on Earth.

Although perhaps only one thousandth of a millimetre in diameter, a typical cell may contain tens of thousands of constituent parts, each essential and each functioning along the biochemical pathways that determine the nature of life. A strand of DNA (deoxyribonucleic acid) stores the blueprint, the hereditary information that ensures exact duplication of everything when the cell divides into two; enzymes direct the cell's biochemical reactions; small particles called ribosomes manufacture proteins (including enzymes); mitochondria break down compounds to release energy; in green plants chloroplasts make sugars with the aid of sunlight ... the structure and functions of the cell are extremely complex, but they all answer to the fundamental logic of chemistry. A cell is made of chemical compounds; its functions are a definable sequence of chemical cause and effect. The DNA molecule defines the cell's nature, but more basic still, proteins are the key to the cell's existence. Proteins make up the structure of the cell, they regulate its processes and in the form of enzymes they catalyze its biochemical reactions. Proteins, in their turn, are made of amino acids, which are molecules composed of carbon, hydrogen, nitrogen and oxygen. Theoretically, a wide variety of amino acids could be formed from these basic ingredients, but in fact only 20 different kinds are used to build proteins. And it is always the same 20, whether in a single-cell bacterium, a leaf cell, or a human cell. So it could be said that amino acids, along with five nitrogenous molecules, plus glucose, some fats and sugars are the basic alphabet that spells out the story of life on Earth. As it happens, there are 29 characters (or compounds) in this basic alphabet of life, just three more than suffice for the English language. These 29 characters do not spell out the whole story, but they do constitute an extraordinarily good opening chapter. Without them there would be no cells; without cells, no life.

Logically it would seem that having identified the 29 characters that compose the alphabet of life, the origin of life has been explained too. But these relatively simple 29 organic compounds, the basis of living matter, for a long time were not known to orginate in anything *but* living matter. Now there's a paradox. If only living organisms can produce the compounds essential for life, how did life begin?

*   *   *

In the 1830s and '40s, while scientists were defining the cell as the basic unit of life, Charles Darwin was already set on the path of enquiry that led inevitably to the theoretical conclusion that the cell was not only the basic unit of life, but the origin of life as well. His theory of evolution by natural selection was carefully expounded in *The Origin of Species*, which was published in 1859 and immediately became the

The emergence of Charles Darwin's 'warm little pond' theory: writing to a colleague in 1871, Darwin speculated on the likelihood of proteins having evolved from inorganic materials on the early Earth.

focus of considerable debate, mainly concerned with the theory's apparent contradiction of the supernatural explanation of life's origins. A decade later, however, the evidence of living organisms and the theory of evolution itself had led many to the expectation that life must have begun long, long ago in a very simple form. Thomas Huxley expressed the sentiment admirably in 1870:

'Looking back through the prodigious vista of the past, I find no record of the commencement of life, and therefore I am devoid of any means of forming a definite conclusion as to the conditions of its appearance. Belief, in the scientific sense of the word, is a serious matter, and needs strong foundations. To say, therefore, in the admitted absence of evidence, that I have any belief as to the mode in which existing forms of life originated, would be using words in a wrong sense. But expectation is permissible where belief is not; and if it were given to me to look beyond the abyss of geologically recorded time to the still more remote period when the Earth was passing through physical and chemical conditions which it can no more see again than a man can recall his infancy, I should expect to be a witness of the evolution of living protoplasm from not living matter.'

The following year Charles Darwin himself gave a very plausible outline of just where the evolution of life from non-living matter might be expected to have taken place:

'. . . if (and oh! what a big if!) we could conceive in some warm little pond, with all sorts of ammonia and phosphoric salts, light, heat, electricity, etc., present, that a protein compound was chemically formed ready to undergo still more complex changes. . . .'

But there the debate halted for some time. The expectation that a fortuitous combination of chemicals, charged with the appropriate amount of energy would form organic compounds that might then become proteins and living cells was confident enough, but no one was able to explain just how it might have happened.

To some extent the problem was that science was still labouring under the old Aristotelian assumption that nothing really changes. There was a general belief that the essentials of life in their broadest terms had always been the same as they are now. This included a dependence on oxygen, and it was well known that although oxygen was essential for the support of life, its presence would oxidize and destroy the simple organic compounds that lay at the origin of life as they were formed, thereby forestalling the establishment of life. Another paradox.

The breakthrough came eventually in the 1920s, when the discoveries of another discipline encouraged biologists to indulge in a piece of simple, but radical rethinking. Astronomers had convincingly shown that the atmospheres of Jupiter and Saturn were composed largely of methane and ammonia, without a trace of free oxygen. What if the same were true of the Earth before the advent of life?

Independently, but following the same train of thought, the Russian biochemist A.I.Oparin (in 1924) and the British biologist J.B.S. Haldane (in 1929) published papers showing how, without oxygen to build the screen of ozone that protects the Earth today, organic compounds could have been created by the effects of the huge amounts of energy provided by the Sun's ultraviolet radiation acting on the primitive atmosphere. More energy would have been provided by the electric storms that must have occurred on the early Earth. Over millions of years the accumulating compounds in the 'warm little pond' would have gathered together in ever more complex form. Eventually, Oparin and Haldane hypothesized, one was formed which possessed the inherent ability to replicate itself, and from that moment life was under way.

Oparin's paper was not translated into English until 1936, and therefore had limited circulation outside the Soviet Union until then. Meanwhile, Haldane's ideas were dismissed as wild speculation – and Oparin's paper met the same fate when it finally reached the West.

This reaction is perhaps not so surprising. Biochemistry was still new territory awaiting exploration at the time. Its participants were busily pushing back the frontiers and mapping the chemical pathways only recently found to be at the heart of living systems. This was exciting and challenging research that offered the promise of positive results. By comparison, the question of origins seemed essentially philosophical and not especially interesting. But its day would come, 20 years later, when the new and exciting research of the 1930s had become the stuff of textbooks that students in the 1950s had to absorb before moving on to research of their own.

*   *   *

If there is one aspect of all scientific endeavour that might strike the enquiring layman as an absolutely essential ingredient of discovery, it must be the element of sheer chance. A glance through the record will turn up any number of scientific discoveries that might not have occurred when they did but for some chance incident. Archimedes' bath was too full (eureka!); the apple was ripe and fell on Newton's head (gravity); Alexander Fleming absent-mindedly neglected one particular culture-dish (penicillin). Similarly, chance ensured that Stanley Miller would be remembered as the man who supplied the first experimental proof of how life might have originated on Earth.

A graduate student of chemistry at the University of Chicago in the early 1950s, Miller planned to write a PhD thesis on how elements might be formed in very hot stars. Six months after he had started his research, chance intervened. Edward Teller, the professor who was guiding Miller's work, left the university, and Miller decided it was impracticable to continue without him. Casting around for a new idea, he eventually decided to test the Oparin/Haldane hypothesis as his PhD topic.

Overleaf: symbols from the contemporary world of high technology and micro-engineering combine to represent the complex chemistry of the events from which life on Earth arose.

21

Miller designed an experiment simulating the conditions thought to have prevailed on the early Earth. Methane and ammonia gases were subjected to electrical discharges while circulating over the surface of a 'warm little pond' of water. After 24 hours of such treatment, about half the carbon originally present in the methane had been converted to amino acids and other organic molecules. The concentration of organic matter produced by the experiment has been described as equalling that of a thin but nourishing chicken broth.

Subsequently, Miller's experiment has been repeated with refinements. It has been shown that virtually any source of energy – lightning, ultraviolet radiation, hot volcanic ash – would have produced complex organic compounds from the materials present on the primitive Earth. Modifications to the experiment itself, along with different mixtures of gases, have produced almost all the common amino acids as well as the nitrogenous bases of which the DNA molecule is composed.

Thus it has been convincingly demonstrated that all 29 characters that make up the basic alphabet of life could have been formed on the primitive Earth by logical and well-understood processes of chemical cause and effect. The consensus opinion goes on from there to hypothesize that as more and more of the 29 characters were formed, the primordial soup thickened, bringing the molecules into closer and closer proximity and subjecting them to the same chemical forces that are known to act on organic molecules today. In concentration, small organic molecules react with each other to form larger and more complex molecules. Under certain conditions some of these will spontaneously form a membrane, or a film on the surface of water, which on being agitated may break up into globules, perhaps enclosing a number of other molecules, cutting them off from the surrounding environment as in a globule of oil in water, although the scale is of course minute. Within the microscopic sphere thus created, chemical reactions will continue among the enclosed molecules, and the spheres have been observed to grow by absorbing material into the membrane from the surrounding soup. As they reach a critical size buds develop and detach themselves to become independent growing microspheres.

These microspheres that scientists have produced experimentally are not alive, but their similarity to living cells is strikingly obvious. If they contain amino acids, the same material of which proteins are made, their internal chemical reactions become analogous to those of a living cell; they divide and multiply in the same manner that living cells employ. This is still a long, long way from the complexity of a living cell, but nonetheless a persuasive indication of just how living cells may have come into being. After all, there must have been many 'warm little ponds' on the early Earth, plenty of energy and vast aeons of time. The production of amino acids and the other organic compounds that comprise the 29 characters of life's basic alphabet would have been continuous. Eventually some came together in a form that endowed the entity thus created with the chemical reactions needed to sustain and reproduce itself.

The ability to reproduce is the ultimate definition of life and although long considered an inexplicable miracle, it is now understood in terms of biochemical cause and effect that occurs within the cell. The hereditary blueprint, DNA, is the secret of it all, and just as biochemists have been able to explain the functioning replicative process of the DNA molecule as a series of chemical reactions, so it has become possible to suggest how the origin of life's vital spark, reproduction, might also have been the result of chemical cause and effect.

The dynamics of all living systems are at root the dynamics of chemical reactions which produce their particular result by tending to favour the survival of some chemical compounds in the reaction rather than others.

These dynamics, and the rates of reaction and survival, vary predictably with varying levels of energy input and environmental circumstance, and David Usher of Cornell University has described how the basic ingredients of the DNA molecule, the nucleotides, could have combined to form the first chains of linked, self-replicating polynucleotides in response to the natural cycle of events on the primitive Earth.

Put at its simplest, the daily round of sunrise and sunset created alternations of light and dark, heat and cold, wet and dry, which acted like a very regular switching on and off of the energy and environmental circumstances affecting the 29 basic characters of life. This on/off effect, heating and cooling, wetting and drying, expanding and contracting, would have broken the chemical bonds of many substances and thereby destroyed them, but it may have favoured the survival of polynucleotide chains that wrapped round each other to form a double helix. This in effect was the most stable configuration under the prevailing circumstances.

Prior to the formation of a double helix the polynucleotides were still random chemical substances, but should two complementary strands meet they would spontaneously form a double helix. Under certain stimuli these two strands would separate, whereupon the chemical nature of each independent strand would attract the compounds needed to build another double helix, and so there would be two where before there had been one. The first self-replicating molecules – DNA.

Although but an assembly of chemical compounds brought together by the on/off, positive/negative dichotomy that lies behind so much of the Earth's functioning, these first DNA molecules were effectively alive. They had taken the logic of chemistry across the threshold from the inanimate to the animate world. Now biology would compound the basic dynamics of the Earth, and evolution would spell out life's story from the 29 characters encoded in the first living cell.

Viewed in the human context, the chemical origin of life on Earth seems to involve an element of chance so huge that it is often quoted as evidence against the probability. Sir Fred Hoyle, for example, puts the odds at billions and billions to one against. He says there is more chance of a man throwing 50,000 consecutive sixes with a pair of dice than there is of the essential molecules combining by chance to form the basis of a living cell. But the trouble with statistics of this kind is that their impact is related to the human lifespan, while the phenomenon of life itself must be seen in an inordinately larger context.

The 29 essential characters were present by the million in every teaspoonful of the waters on the primitive Earth, and there was not just one lifespan available for their chance combination, there were a hundred million lifespans. On this scale, odds of billions to one against are not at all unreasonable. And it only had to happen once. From the moment that some of the 29 characters spelled out the first word, the first living cell, the logic of biochemistry took over the composition of life's story. The first self-sustaining, self-replicating living cell would not have been alone for long. Two, then four, eight, sixteen ... doubling with every generation; the potential was enormous and the known principles of biology, life systems and evolution make it possible to understand how the entire living world is derived from the first single cell. Once the process had begun, its progress is not difficult to follow.

* * *

There is no doubt that life was born of the materials that comprise the Earth, the stars and the universe. The same materials, recycled over and over again throughout timeless space. In the end we are all stardust. Just as life evolved from the single cell to ever more complex and diverse forms, so the Earth has evolved too: condensing from an aggregation of inter-stellar dust, cooling to a globe with a solid crust nearly four billion years ago, but even to this day subject to the forces of its internal heat.

An appreciation of the Earth's story was already well developed by the time Darwin proposed a warm little pond as a site for the origin of life. Geology, the science of the Earth, had long recognized that the layers of rock – the strata – could be identified by their mineral characteristics and, in the case of sedimentary rocks, also by the fossils they contained. The strata had been named, their order of deposition and the age of one in relation to another had been established. It had been possible to correlate some sequences with others from around the world and a picture of the Earth's changing form was taking shape.

Sedimentary rocks, which cover more than two-thirds of the Earth's surface, provided a wealth of information concerning the shifting coastlines and the changing climates of the past, and the fossil remains of plants and animals preserved within the sediments were regarded as a unique record of the progression of life on Earth. When Darwin published his theory of evolution in 1859 it was immediately recognized that fossils could be a means of testing it. If life had evolved through time from simple to more complex and diverse forms, as Darwin claimed, then fossils should show a similar degree of evolution through the ascending layers of sedimentary rocks. Fossils in the most

26

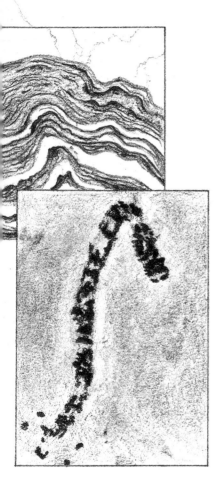

Revelations in the rocks: microscopic cells (bottom), fossilized in samples from the Canadian Gunflint Formation (below and left), show that a variety of single-cell organisms were already in existence more than two billion years ago.

recent rocks should be the most complex; those in the most ancient should be the simplest. And was it possible that the fossil record might go back to the beginning of life?

The question was resolved many years after Darwin's death. In the early 1950s, Stanley Tyler, a geologist from the University of Wisconsin, and Elso Barghoorn, a botanist at Harvard, discovered conclusive evidence of single-cell organisms in samples of Canadian rock that had been laid down at an early stage in the Earth's creation.

Using the newly developed radiometric dating procedures, Tyler and Barghoorn identified four distinct forms of single-cell organism, two algae and two fungi, along with one indeterminate form. They were all extremely small, only thousandths of a millimetre long, but they were well preserved and similar to the simplest known organisms living today; they were close, therefore, to the origin of life.

With the refinement of radiometric dating procedures bringing even greater precision to age estimates for the ancient rocks, and with electron microscopes resolving ever-finer detail in the fossils found in the rocks, it began to seem that perhaps at last the tantalizing question could be answered: with what, and when, did life on Earth begin?

With the nicety that science reserves for expressing degrees of uncertainty the evidence has been rated in terms of the possible, the probable and the definite.

The oldest *possible* evidence of life is a number of cell-like inclusions found in rocks from Isua, Greenland, that had been dated at 3·8 billion years old, around 800 million years after the Earth's crust had formed. Some said this was much too soon for life to have had time to evolve from raw chemicals, and among the doubters Sir Fred Hoyle held the Isua specimens as convincing evidence that life must have come to Earth from elsewhere. But the evidence of cell-like structures in the Isua rocks was not incontrovertible. Organic origin was questioned, and the rocks seemed to have been subjected to so much heat since their formation that there was little chance that microfossils would have been preserved in them even if there had been micro-organisms there in the first place. So most authorities rate the Isua specimens as at best only possibly the earliest evidence of life on Earth.

The best *probable* evidence comes from 3·5-billion-year-old rocks in the Pilbara Block in Australia and the Barberton Mountain Land in Swaziland. Here microfossils have been found in rocks that showed none of the heat effect that clouded the evidence from Isua.

The oldest *definite* evidence of life on Earth is the 2·7-billion-year-old fossils from Slave Province and Steep Rock Lake in Canada. These are superbly preserved and unquestionably of organic origin since they precisely duplicate details of the simplest living single-cell organisms, especially those from Shark Bay in Western Australia which have been extensively studied in recent years.

Meanwhile, the rocks from which Tyler and Barghoorn took their samples have been dated at a mere two billion years old, but in the course of over 20 years of study they have provided a compelling picture of the status of life at that very distant stage.

CYANOBACTERIA
Nostoc sp. 80x mag.
(Colour enhanced)

Photograph by
Sinclair Stammers
Copyright 1986

Chapter Two

OXYGEN

a breath of life

The creation of the atmosphere that swirls around the Earth today began more than 2 billion years ago when microscopic aquatic cyanobacteria, probably very similar to the modern *Nostoc* (left), released oxygen as a by-product of photosynthesis. Oxygen produced by cyanobacteria also precipitated dissolved iron from the oceans, laying down the banded ironstone (slab at rear) which today comprises most of the world's economic iron reserves.

For convenience of description and reference science has divided its account of the Earth's history into four broad sections called eras, and named each according to the status of life at the time – as revealed by the fossil record. Going back from the present the eras are: the Cenozoic, meaning recent life; the Mesozoic, middle life; the Paleozoic, early life, and the Precambrian, which was known as the Azoic – without trace of life – until it was discovered that life had existed even then.

By far the greatest part of the information available on the Earth and life comes from the Cenozoic era; less comes from the Mesozoic, even less from the Paleozoic, and least of all from the Precambrian. And yet the Precambrian encompasses nearly 90 per cent of the Earth's history, stretching from 4·5 billion years ago, when the Earth condensed to become a solid planet, to 570 million years ago, when the fossil evidence first reveals living cells combined in the form of multicellular organisms.

The Precambrian era – so vast, so distant, so veiled by the knowledge of more recent times – is easiest to imagine in terms of what it lacked, like a distant empty desert lying beyond the consciousness of a dynamic city.

But deserts have their dynamics too. For the first thousand million years or so of the Precambrian era these dynamics were simply the physical forces of the planet itself, but once some enigmatic molecules had acquired the knack of replicating themselves around 3·5 billion years ago, the process of life became the dynamic force most responsible for the way the Earth looks today. Without the advent of life the Earth would have taken on an entirely different aspect – most probably resembling that of the Moon, or of Mars.

The effects of life on the Earth have been accumulative, but slow moving. For the best part of its first 2·5 billion years life would have been microscopic in scale. A host of organisms, each barely one thousandth of a millimetre in diameter, teeming through the oceans and all the 'warm little ponds' of the world.

The fossil record provides firm evidence that single-cell organisms have existed on Earth for a very long time, and gives an idea of their increasing size, shape and functional complexity through time, but the story of their evolutionary development from single cell to more complex organism comes largely from the evidence of modern living organisms.

All living things share four fundamental and inter-related characteristics: they are all cellular in structure; the protein in all cells is made up from basically the same 20 amino acid units; all cells use basically the same nucleotides in their genes; and all cells use ATP (adenosine triphosphate) as the molecule that energizes their life systems. These four characteristics are in effect a definition of life. Each is a very complex phenomenon and that they should be common to every living thing from microbe to man cannot be an accident. Such universality can only result from a common origin. It must mean that all living things have evolved from a single ancestral form. And that ancestral form was probably very similar to the smallest and simplest organisms alive on Earth today.

The smallest and simplest living things are single-cell organisms with a simple DNA molecule (their genetic material) floating free within the cell. Since these cells do not keep their DNA in a separate enclosed nucleus, they are called prokaryotes, from the Greek *pro*, meaning 'before', and *karyon*, meaning 'kernel' or 'nucleus'. Prokaryotes are the most widely dispersed living things, inhabiting environments of all sorts – from the depths of the oceans to the vents of volcanoes; from the Polar ice-caps to the near boiling water of natural hot springs. Some can remain frozen, or desiccated, or otherwise dormant for years and return to life afterwards as though nothing had happened. Others can survive several hours of boiling in water.

Among the prokaryotes, the very simplest are a group called the methanogens, bacteria which are found in marshes, lake beds and the digestive tracts of animals. The methanogens have been known for a long time but they were not studied extensively until the 1970s – mainly because oxygen is poisonous to them, which made it impossible to rear them under ordinary laboratory conditions. Studies were eventually instigated, however, and it became known that the methanogens are members of a small and exclusive group of organisms that are able to live off inorganic chemicals without the aid of any other source of energy. In the process they give off methane, marsh gas. The life process employed by the methanogens is called fermentation, well known as the means of leavening bread and making alcohol – prokaryotic bacteria are the active fermenting agents in both cases.

Two other kinds of bacteria that have the capacity to live off inorganic chemicals under extreme conditions are the halobacteria that live in very salty environments, and the thermoacidophiles, which thrive in hot acidic environments. These three kinds of bacteria would have been well equipped for life in the harsh environments that prevailed on the early Earth, when there was no oxygen in the atmosphere but plenty of heat and inorganic chemicals about. They could be survivors of a lineage that arose then. Certainly the methanogens and their kind can be considered good analogues for the forms of life that existed on Earth at the earliest stages of evolution.

The inorganic chemical-consuming bacteria had the early Earth all to themselves for some considerable time – hundreds of millions of years. Eventually the materials they took from the environment to build and energize themselves would have been finished, and at that point life on Earth might have come to a lingering end. But the crisis was avoided, in fact it was never even a threat, because from the beginning life has been ruled by its inherent capacity to adapt and change as the environment dictates. The cell form, the amino acids, the ATP and the DNA remain the same, but their arrangements are adapted to take advantage of new circumstances. There is nothing conscious or directed, or even survival-oriented about the procedure. It is simply a matter of the chance mutations between generations producing individual organisms that are better suited than their antecedents to the changing environment. The mutants and their offspring thrive. The old guard either becomes extinct or retreats to some place where the environment has remained unchanged – this process is called natural selection. Thus the dinosaurs disappeared off the face of the Earth following the climatic changes that occurred 65 million years ago, and the methanogens and their kind are found living today only in very special circumstances.

Adaptive change is the basis of evolutionary theory. Evolution is not a fight for survival as is often supposed, with success meaning the direct elimination of competing organisms. It is a process by which new organisms and systems constantly arise to exploit new resources and opportunities.

Mutation is the key factor. Experiments have shown that by the time a culture of the modern prokaryote *Escherichia coli* (an inhabitant of the human gut and similar environments) has divided 30 times, no less than 1.5 per cent of its number are mutants. And the generation times can be very short; given ideal conditions *E. coli* can double in number every 20 minutes.

So, with the densities of their living populations probably exceeding millions of cells per cubic centimetre, and with the passage of millions of years, the methanogens and their kind must have come up with

Simple reproduction, frozen in time — fossil cells from the Bitter Springs Formation in Australia are thought to be evidence of cell division that occurred 850 million years ago.

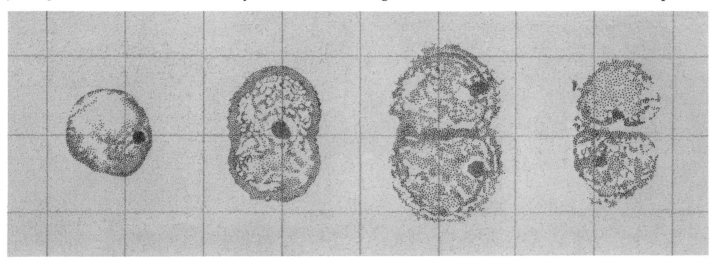

countless mutations during the first few hundred million years of life on Earth. Quite early on these would have produced organisms variously adapted to thrive in every environment that the Earth had to offer. But the process did not stop there. Eventually, somewhere among the teeming microscopic hordes, mutation produced an organism that was able to harness the radiant energy of the Sun to its life processes. This was an innovation of immense significance that has marked the course of life ever since.

The principle was that instead of using chemicals absorbed from its surroundings both as the materials needed for growth *and* as the fuel to process those materials, as every prokaryote had done until then, the new mutant used the energy of sunlight to power its life processes. Energy coming in from outside left more available inside, with the consequence that the organism was more energy-efficient than its antecedents. Life now had the means to exploit a widened realm of resources. There has always been plenty of sunlight – harnessing it to life is called photosynthesis.

The essence of photosynthesis is the ability to convert the energy of light to another form, and this ability is related to the phenomenon of colour. Black objects warm up very quickly when exposed to sunlight because they convert all the light striking them into heat; white objects remain cool because they reflect all the light that strikes them; red objects warm up just to the extent that they absorb yellow and blue light, blue objects to the extent that they absorb yellow and red light, and so on, through all the colours of the spectrum and the intensities of light energy that they represent. Put at its simplest, colour is a visual representation of the energy left over when an object has absorbed all that it is tuned to take from the visible spectrum.

Studies of light and colour and of how photosynthesis works in organisms living today – from the simplest to the most complex – have provided the evidence for a hypothesis explaining how photosynthesis may have evolved on the early Earth.

In the course of those countless mutations, some prokaryotes evolved with the capacity to produce and use porphyrins in their life processes. Porphyrins are light-absorbing compounds; their advent and incorporation in living matter was probably fortuitous, so too perhaps was the fact that they were coloured. Until then life had been colourless, but now among the millions of organisms there were, for the first time, microscopic grains of colour that today are called chlorophyll – the wonder ingredient that takes light from the Sun and converts it into a tiny bank of energy in the core of the cell. The first chlorophylls were probably purplish – some living forms among the simplest bacteria still are – but they have subsequently evolved into a variety of other hues as well, including the numerous shades of green that colour the Earth today.

Photosynthesis requires a source of hydrogen. The first photosynthesizers would have taken this very basic ingredient from the compound molecules they absorbed from the water around them, just as their antecedents had done. But time and evolution brought further refinement. Eventually, about three billion years ago, an organism arose that was able to absorb hydrogen direct by splitting the water molecule into its component parts: two parts hydrogen and one part oxygen. The hydrogen was used in photosynthesis; the oxygen was released as waste.

It is thought likely that these first photosynthesizers lived mostly in dense, mat-like communities on the floor of shallow seas. Diversifying, limited only by the balance between water shallow enough to allow them sufficient light but deep enough to protect them from the destructive effects of the Sun's ultraviolet radiation, the photosynthesizing prokaryotes spread around the Earth. By around 2·2 billion years ago they were the dominant life-form, and the oxygen they released as waste began to have telling effects.

There was no oxygen in the atmosphere surrounding the early Earth, indeed the gas would have been lethal to all its first inhabitants. Experiments have shown that even the chemical processes that formed the first amino acids and other organic compounds in the 'warm little pond' could not have occurred if there had been even very small concentrations of molecular oxygen around. It seems certain that life as we know it could not have arisen in the presence of oxygen; and yet today life could not exist without it. How has this paradox come about?

In the early days the oxygen given off by the photosynthesizers would have been only a very small drop in the ocean – literally. The small amounts produced would have been dispersed and chemically neutralized before they could have much effect on the surroundings. But the trend towards an oxygenated environment had been set. Millions of years passed. The photosynthesizers proliferated slowly, but eventually the amounts of oxygen they were giving off approached critical levels. Until that moment the evolution of life had been subject to only the physical characteristics of the Earth – life had adapted to the environment – but now life itself became a formative factor. With the advent of oxygen life began to change the face of the Earth.

From among the diverse variety of single-cell organisms then existing, the methanogens and their kind retreated to the oxygen-free muds and other places similar to the habitats in which their descendants still flourish; any organisms that found no safe haven became extinct. Among the photosynthesizers natural selection favoured forms that could tolerate increasing concentrations of oxygen.

Meanwhile, the increasing amount of oxygen released by the photosynthesizers was also bringing about considerable changes to the environment. In the first instance it turned the oceans rusty.

Iron is a major component of the Earth. In the absence of oxygen it can exist in a soluble state, and the early oceans would have contained huge quantities of dissolved iron. But once the concentration of oxygen in the oceans reached a critical level, it began to react with the dissolved iron, forming iron oxides, which are insoluble. The iron oxides were precipitated out of solution and sank to the ocean floor.

In the relatively short space of 200 million years or so, billions of tonnes of iron oxides were laid down on ocean floors around the world. The deposits are remarkably regular in form, but they are not solid masses, they are made up of bands of iron oxide lying between bands of a red, silica-rich rock. The iron bands vary in thickness from a few millimetres to several centimetres. In section the bands of iron-grey and red give the rock a most distinctive appearance and the deposits have been named the Banded Ironstone Formations.

The banded nature of the deposits must surely be related to a pattern of increase and decrease of numbers among the photosynthesizers themselves. During warmer periods there were more photosynthesizers at work, producing more oxygen, precipitating more iron. In cooler periods their numbers would have declined, and for a time silica and other materials (including the remains of dead photosynthesizers) were the dominant components of the accumulating deposits. And so it went on for millions of years.

Eventually, the oxygen produced by the microscopic photosynthesizers swept the oceans clean of iron. Now for the first time free oxygen escaped from the oceans and began to accumulate in the atmosphere. This development brought further irreversible change to the environment of life on Earth.

Oxygen was becoming a fact of life. Many more oxygen-tolerant forms had arisen, and some had even gone so far as to add a few molecules of oxygen to the fermentation process that alone had powered life until then. The result was very beneficial to the organisms concerned, releasing 18 times more energy than fermentation alone could release from the same amount of material. In effect the innovators held on to the waste product of fermentation and combined it with oxygen for another round of energy-producing reactions. This is called cellular respiration; basically it is why we breathe.

The respirators used the available resources more efficiently than any of their predecessors. They proliferated. At the same time there came the single-cell cyanobacteria (also known as the blue-green algae), still very small but more inclined to a communal life than anything that had come before. The cyanobacteria joined themselves together end-to-end to form strands of green living matter.

Photosynthesizers, respirators and cyanobacteria were now the dominant life-forms, churning out more and more oxygen, but still confined to those bands of water shallow enough to transmit sufficient sunlight for their life processes, and deep enough to filter out the Sun's lethal ultraviolet radiation. For some time the progression of life on Earth seems to have halted at this critical point of balance between the good and the bad effects of the Sun.

Some sort of evolutionary innovation might have been the device most expected to break the impasse, but in the event it was not needed. Life was finally released from the tyranny of the ultraviolet rays by the indirect effects of life itself. Without doubt this was one of the most significant interactions between life and the global environment that has ever occurred. Once again the active agent was oxygen.

Like so much else, oxygen gas is susceptible to the destructive effects of sunlight. When subjected to intense solar radiation the gaseous

Cellular evolution on the early Earth proceeded by chance mutation along pathways laid down by the immutable laws of physics and chemistry.

34

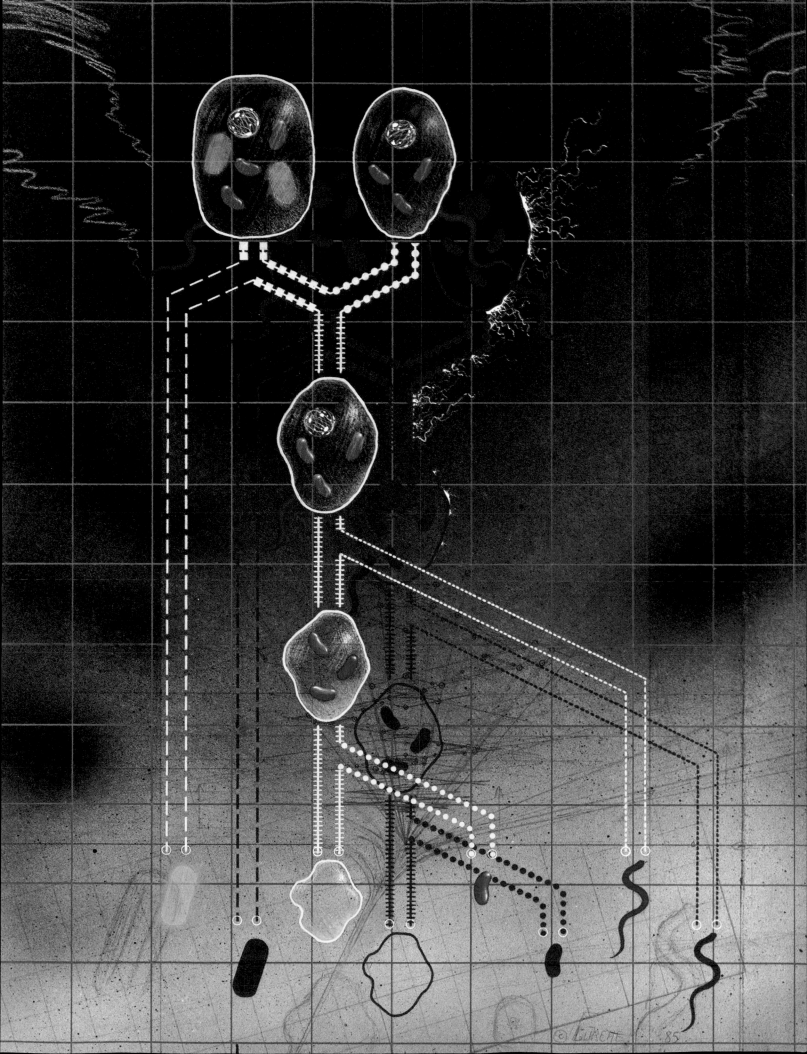

oxygen molecule O_2 is split into two single oxygen atoms, some of which get together in groups of three to form the O_3 molecule, which is another gas called ozone, and ozone has the capacity of absorbing ultraviolet radiation.

The process was continuous, ozone accumulating above the oxygen as it escaped from the oceans. And as the ozone layer thickened, life could move closer and closer to the surface of the water; it could even, perhaps, survive for a time where warm little ponds had dried out completely. The surfaces of water and land presented new habitats, new opportunities for the evolution of life and, as is abundantly clear from the state of the Earth today, they were not neglected. Furthermore, evolutionary development took a great leap forward at this stage: after the prokaryotes had been in existence for possibly two billion years, a major transition took place, hardly of less significance than the origin of life itself – a new type of cell appeared.

The fossil record shows that until about 1·45 billion years ago prokaryotic cells were the only living forms. The prokaryotes had carried life from its very beginnings to a state of really quite advanced diversity. They laid the ground-plan of life and set the environmental scene for all that it has produced – and then their development stopped. The prokaryotes living today are still the smallest and the simplest organisms that life has ever known. Every other living thing has come into being through the medium of another kind of cell, the eukaryote (*eu* meaning 'true').

The four fundamentals of life – cellular structure, amino acids for proteins, DNA for genes, and ATP for energy transmission – link the eukaryotes and the prokaryotes as surely as a flower to its stem. The evidence of the fossil record leaves no doubt that the prokaryotes came first, and this conclusion is further supported by the evidence from living organisms, amongst whom it is found that although the prokaryotes are variably tolerant of oxygen – all the way from being unable to live *with* it to being unable to live *without* it – virtually all the eukaryotes have an absolute need of oxygen, and even the exceptions seem to be descendants of oxygen-dependent forms. All this leads to the conclusion that the eukaryotes must have arisen after the oceans and the atmosphere had been oxygenated by the prokaryotes.

However, although the evidence strongly suggests that the eukaryotes must have evolved from the prokaryotes, the differences between the two groups are of a scale that seems to call for more than just time and mutation to have brought forth the really rather complex eukaryotes from the so much simpler prokaryotes.

The eukaryote cell is generally larger, with several distinct parts, called organelles, within the cell, and their genetic material is contained within a nucleus, where it is associated with protein structures known as chromosomes. A typical eukaryote has about 1,000 times more DNA than any prokaryote and this has an important bearing on its mode of reproduction and its evolutionary potential.

Prokaryote reproduction is conducted by the relatively simple procedure of binary fission. First the DNA is replicated, then the cell elongates, pinches in the middle and divides, leaving two cells, each containing a copy of the original DNA.

In eukaryotes reproduction is essentially a process of division too, but it is rendered much more complex by the number of different elements and larger quantities involved. Each organelle has to be duplicated and apportioned, and as the nucleus divides each part must receive exactly the right number of chromosomes. Sometimes the component parts of the genetic material may be slightly reshuffled, so that duplication is not necessarily exact. The complexity of their reproductive process broadens the potential effects of mutation in eukaryote cells.

So how did the eukaryotes come into being? The most plausible hypothesis yet put forward to explain their origin suggests that the evolutionary development involved may have been more behavioural than physical. The idea is that it was not so much alterations to the prokaryote cell as such that created the eukaryotes, rather that some among them began to behave differently, living together in a mutually beneficial relationship that is common enough in the living world today, called symbiosis.

The hypothesis suggests that the eukaryote organelles were once independent cells that evolved the behavioural capacity to enter and live inside another prokaryote, and subsequently became part of a give-and-take relationship that bestowed benefits on both parties. This explanation was first mooted in the nineteenth century. It surfaced again in the 1920s, in a book by an American physician, J.E. Wallin, but achieved more notoriety than support when it was found that Wallin had fudged his experiments and distorted the data. In the 1970s the role of symbiosis in the evolution of the eukaryote cell was examined again by Lynn Margulis of Boston University. As a result of her work the suggestion that organelles were once independent organisms has gained in credibility.

The hypothesis is strongly supported by evidence from the living world. Lichen, for instance, is actually algae and fungus living together in a symbiotic relationship. The photosynthesizing algae fuel the partnership while the fungus provides a home base and security. Together the partners can inhabit a far wider range of environments and live much longer than either could alone. Scientists have demonstrated the symbiotic nature of the lichens by separating their algal and fungal components, and rearing them independently, but the partners have been together for so long that their symbiosis is now hereditary. The algae and fungi do not have to find each other with each generation as their earliest antecedents must have done; when they reproduce, the symbiotic lichen is produced – ready-made.

Hereditary symbiosis such as the lichens have developed occurs in other organisms too. There is a green plant, *Psychotria bacteriophila*, for instance, whose seeds contain not only the genetic material and other essential material usually passed on from one generation to the next, but also a batch of the symbiotic bacteria the plant must have at its roots to convert atmospheric nitrogen to a form the plant can utilize.

Yet more complex is the case of *Myxotricha paradoxa*, a single-cell organism that has found a home in the gut of certain Australian termites, where it feeds itself and at the same time performs the essential task of releasing the nutrients that nourish its host. The small termites eat dead wood, but they could not survive without the microscopic *Myxotricha* in their gut to help them digest it.

Myxotricha acquired the name *paradoxa* because it swims in an unusual and puzzling way. A joint study by A.V. Grimstone of Cambridge University and L.R. Cleveland of the University of Georgia has solved the puzzle of how it swims and shows that *Myxotricha* may itself be the key to the solution of yet other puzzles.

The hair-like appendages called flagella and cilia that propel *Myxotricha* are in fact independent bacteria of an elongated form, living symbiotically on the surface of their host. Somehow, in fulfilling their life processes, they drive *Myxotricha* where it needs to go. Lynn Margulis believes that something like the symbiotic relationship that *Myxotricha* has developed was the origin of the eukaryote cell.

She suggests that as oxygen began to accumulate around the Earth a fermenting bacterium would have found considerable advantage in taking on some smaller respirators as symbiotic partners, and natural selection would have favoured the trend. With time the symbiosis would have become hereditary and a new kind of organism evolved. Meanwhile smaller, more mobile single cells discovered the advantage of living in close association with larger organisms – much as pilot fish align themselves with sharks. Eventually that association too became symbiotic. The smaller organisms attached themselves to their larger partners and became their means of propulsion – the flagella and cilia. Again, the association brought considerable advantage to both parties and the symbiosis eventually became hereditary. So through time, with mutation and evolution, some simple single-cell prokaryotes became first the symbionts of other larger prokaryotes and then the organelles of the ancestral eukaryote. Margulis believes it may have taken one billion years to perfect the eukaryote cell. And the perfect eukaryote cell is the foundation upon which the living world is built.

Standing tall, sharing the Earth with trees, elephants, whales and so many other living things, large and small, it may seem perverse to insist that the perfection of life is represented by the miroscopic eukaryote cell that arose in the primordial seas some 1·45 billion years ago, but it is a fact. In a sense nothing has changed since then; the Earth is still populated by prokaryote and eukaryote cells. The only difference is that while the prokaryotes have remained largely invisible, the eukaryotes have assembled themselves into some impressively visible structures. How has this come about?

The fossil evidence of the eukaryotes' early development gives some clues to its timing and progress. Measurements of some 8,000 fossil cells from 18 Precambrian locations around the world have shown that all cells from rocks older than 1·45 billion years are within the size range of modern prokaryotes. Then there is a distinct jump; cells larger than modern prokaryotes become increasingly abundant, and there is

Symbiosis – the mutual dependence of two living forms – is a common and significant feature of life. The microscopic symbiont, *Myxotricha paradoxa* (top), inhabits the intestinal tract of certain Australian termites, where it aids the digestion of dead wood. The discovery that *Myxotricha* in its turn supports a population of independent bacteria (centre and bottom), which help it move around, is seen as convincing evidence of symbiosis as the origin of the eukaryote cell.

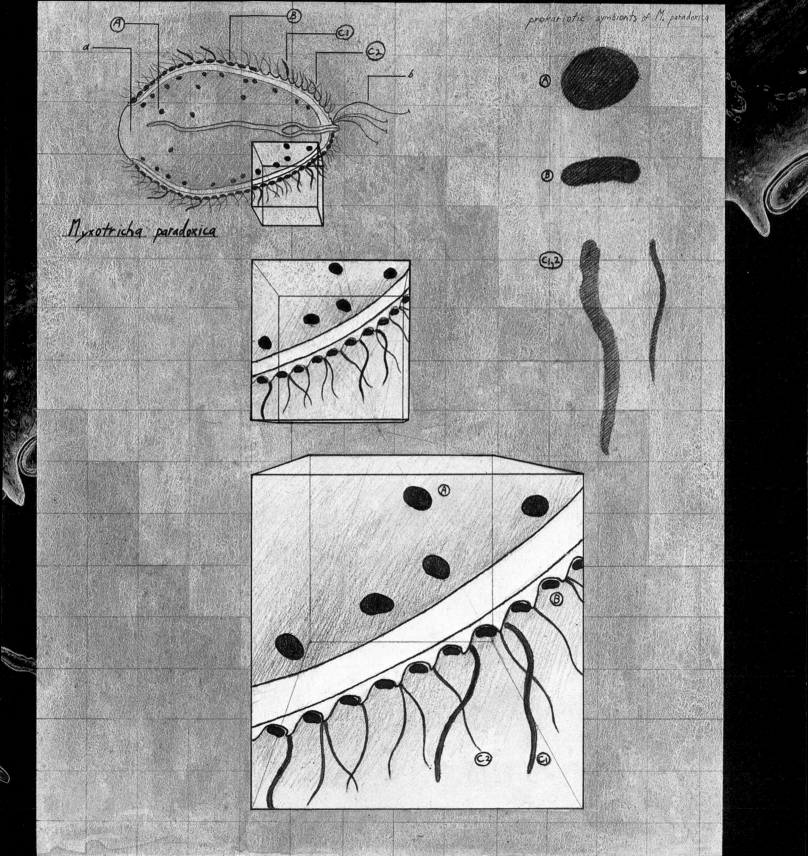

prokariotic symbionts of M. paradoxica

Myxotricha paradoxica

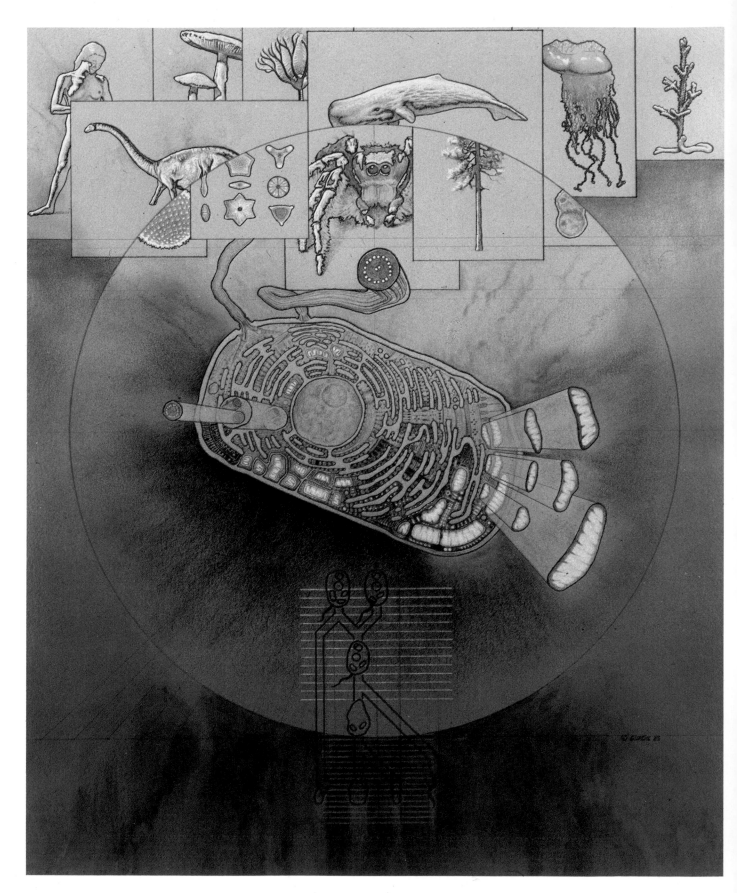

40

evidence of increasingly complex structure and internal organization among these larger microfossils.

Filaments of large cells have come from rocks in California that are more than 1·2 billion years old; spiny cells of unquestionable eukaryote affinity have been found in Siberian shales 950 million years old, and cells containing small dense bodies thought to be preserved organelles have come from formations in central Australia that are about 850 million years old.

It is thought likely that the eukaryotes began to reproduce sexually around one billion years ago. This was an especially significant innovation for, by sharing the genetic material of two parents among the offspring, both the chance of mutation and the potential degree of mutation between generations was increased. In effect, sexual reproduction enhanced the mechanism by which evolution operates and thereby accelerated the process. Increased diversity and proliferation of life-forms was inevitable.

Meanwhile, lifestyles were changing too. For a long time all the single-cell inhabitants of the Earth's seas fed off the same, basically chemical, resources of the planet. Eventually, however, some began to eat others and predation began. Here was a particularly dynamic force that could well have accelerated the evolutionary process still further. Predation brought advantage to the predators and applied strong selection pressure on their prey. Some prey populations probably became extinct; others evolved avoidance equipment or strategies. Among other things, the advent of predation in the story of life may have encouraged some cells to find refuge inside larger cells, where they eventually became the symbionts of the eukaryote cell.

At the same time the concentration of oxygen in the atmosphere was slowly but steadily increasing. The scene was ripe with potential: after some 2·5 billion years life was at last poised to move beyond the microscopic stage of its existence. The key to this step was the advent of the multicellular organism, when some cells developed the characteristic of living together as a colony of cells that itself was a distinct organism, bestowing advantages of nutrition, security and mobility on each of its component parts.

The oldest known multicellular fossil comes from deposits that are about 750 million years old, but their evolution probably began before then. With time and mutation and the pressure of natural selection, some component cells evolved special functions or features that were specific to themselves but beneficial to the whole. New organisms arose, creating and exploiting new opportunities in environments that were becoming increasingly interactive with life itself.

Once the trend was set its progress was inexorable, perhaps even inevitable, but the cellular diversity required to produce the modern living world is not as great as might be supposed. The human body, for instance, is composed of millions upon millions of individual cells, but among them there are hardly more than 100 different kinds of cell. And every single one is a variation on that microscopic, self-sustaining unit – the eukaryote cell.

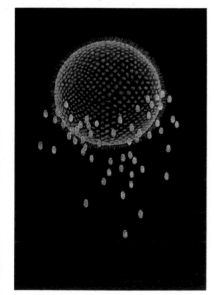

41

Chapter Three

PRIMORDIAL OCEANS

source of all diversity

In the early 19th century the fossilized remains of thousands of marine creatures were chiselled out of the rocks. The systematic study of fossil fish was initiated by the brilliant young Swiss paleontologist, Louis Agassiz.

Sponges, though useful in the bath and existing as some 5,000 distinct species that range in size from the microscopic to the monstrous, are essentially very simple organisms, little more than water-filtering systems made up of one or more chambers through which water flows, carrying nutrients direct to every single cell in the sponge. And since each cell feeds individually, even the largest sponge consumes only microscopic particles.

Structurally, the sponges stand somewhere between a colony of independent cells and true multicellular organisms. They consist of relatively few cell types, there are no distinct tissues or organs, yet the individual cells comprising the organisms do seem to possess some sort of mutual recognition and purpose that enables them to get together and build a sponge. In this respect, sponges are a wonderful example of the single cell as the basis of higher life-forms.

Along the east coast of America, from Nova Scotia all the way down to South Carolina, the elusive oyster beds betray their presence in summer and autumn with occasional patches of bright tomato red. The colour fades away in the winter, returning the following summer. The cause of the colour is a small sponge, known to science as *Microciona prolifera*, which starts out as a thin encrustation on the shells of oysters and eventually grows into a branching, bush-like structure up to 20 centimetres high. The annual colour change is associated with repro-duction.

In the summer of 1907, the biologist H.V. Wilson was working at Beaufort Harbour, North Carolina, on his research into the generation and regeneration of tissue. Among several experiments he conducted that summer, one is of compelling interest.

Wilson collected a bright red living *Microciona prolifera* sponge and cut it up into tiny pieces. Then he put the pieces in a muslin bag which he suspended in a dish of filtered sea water. He shook the bag about and squeezed it gently with a pair of forceps. Clouds of red cells passed through the muslin and into the water. Soon the bag was all but empty and the red sponge had been reduced to a fine sediment on the bottom of the dish.

Wilson watched closely. Within an hour the tiny component cells of the sponge began to gather together in clumps. After a while thin protrusions grew from the clumps and reached through the water, like arms; when they touched another arm, or another clump of cells, the two groups fused into one larger clump, and so the process went on until eventually all the cells were fused together in a single crusted mass on the bottom of the dish. At this point the most amazing thing happened. The cells began to sort out their individual roles in the formation of a sponge and moved to take up position accordingly. As the days went by small open chambers appeared in the crusted surface, canals formed between them and the branching vent tubes began to grow, slowly at first and then rapidly, as though the cells had regained confidence in their collective existence. Within a week the sponge that Wilson had reduced to a fine red sediment was completely rebuilt.

Later, Wilson tried the same experiment on a member of the jellyfish family that has a more complex structure than the sponge, with two distinct layers of tissue. Here too the animal that Wilson cut apart and squeezed through his muslin bag re-formed itself from the disassociated cells.

Sponges represent the lowest form of multicellular development in animals; indeed, for a long time they were not considered to be wholly animal at all and were classified as zoophytes – 'animal plants'. They are also among the most ancient; fossil evidence traces their existence back to the last part of the Precambrian, 700 million years ago. Thus sponges bridge the gap between the world of the microscopic single cell and the world of multicellular higher organisms, but here their contribution to the story of life on Earth ends. Sponges have remained essentially the same ever since; having found their niche, no further evolutionary development occurred.

The mainline story of life, leading from the single cell to the first multicellular organisms, and on to the first backbone, the first fish, the first land animals, the first mammals and so on to man, continues with the single cells that gathered together to form quite different creatures – the soft-bodied jellyfishes and flatworms. Wilson's experiments provided solid enough support for the contention that jellyfishes and their kind must have played an important role in the early evolution of higher multicellular organisms, but the contention was based on theory only and tangible fossil evidence proving their existence at that stage in the story of life was not forthcoming. This was hardly surprising, given the soft-bodied nature of the living animal. After all, who would expect to find a fossil jellyfish? And since no one expected to find any, no one looked for them. Discovery, when and if it came, would yet again be a matter of chance.

*   *   *

By the 1870s the era of geographic exploration in North America was long past; the broad details of the land, lakes, rivers and mountains were known and mapped from coast to coast, but the finer details still

Sea pens, jellyfish and worm-like creatures such as *Dickinsonia* and *Spriggina* (on sea floor) are among the earliest multicellular organisms for which fossil evidence exists. Rare fossil impressions of these and other soft-bodied animals found in the Ediacara Sandstones of southern Australia constitute the oldest animal community on record.

awaited definition. Fortune-seekers wanted a hint of where the next gold strike might be; industrialists urged geologists to seek out workable coal and iron deposits; academics wanted to find new areas of research in their subjects. So when surveyors mapping a route through the Rocky Mountains for the proposed Canadian Pacific Railway sent back word of fantastic mountain peaks, glaciers, lakes and forests in the previously little-known region of the high Burgess Pass, they caught the attention of many interested parties. Among them was George Dawson of the Canadian Geological Survey, who proceeded to make a preliminary study of the area in the early 1880s. He was followed in 1886 by another geologist who described sandstone, shale and limestone deposits thousands of metres thick, dissected and laid bare by uplifting and erosion. Meanwhile the mention of glaciers attracted the attention of George Vaux from Philadelphia, who initiated the first glaciological studies of the region and was assisted in the mountains by his sister, Mary. Mary Vaux married Charles Dolittle Walcott (1850–1927), a paleontologist who was to become world famous for his discoveries in the Burgess Pass region.

In a series of expeditions between 1910 and 1917 Walcott defined a sequence of nearly 4,000 metres of sedimentary rock laid down during the Cambrian period between 570 and 500 million years ago. Over 40,000 fossils were collected from the sequence, among which Walcott described some 150 species belonging to 119 genera. All this can be found in a couple of thousand pages of scientific publications, but the most interesting, and possibly the most significant, aspects of Walcott's work concerned a thin band, about one metre thick, of fossil-bearing shale that he discovered on the south-western flank of Mount Wapta, 2,440 metres above sea level.

Charles D. Walcott was a self-made man in the best American tradition. From relatively humble beginnings, with little formal education, he scaled the heights of science and society in the United States. He was born and grew up in Oneida County, New York State, and liked to recount how his scientific career began there one day in the 1860s when he was a boy riding on the back of a wagon going from Trenton Falls to Trenton. The road was still rough in those days, and as the horse was heaving the wagon out of a dry river crossing, a wheel rode up over a loose block of sandstone and split it clean open. As the fragments shot away from the wheel, young Charles Walcott looked round and caught a glimpse of what had been trapped in the sandstone for hundreds of millions of years – a fossil trilobite, beautifully preserved. He jumped down to pick it up, and his passion for collecting fossils began right there.

Soon after, Walcott took a job in a Trenton hardware store, and spent most of his spare time collecting and reading, especially about the Cambrian rock systems in Europe. His ambition was to study the Cambrian systems in America, then still undefined, but first he wanted to study geology and paleontology at Harvard University. It took him until he was 23 to save up enough money to pay for his college course,

The trilobites were a diverse and highly specialized group of organisms. The fossilized remains of their hard external skeletons provide ample evidence of their existence in the oceans around 550 million years ago (right). In the sponge colony beneath them are a worm-like onychophoran (left), a pair of shelled brachiopods, a snail and a trilobitomorph.

but once he began his studies he soon made his first significant contribution to science with some distinctive work on the trilobites he had collected around Trenton.

Trilobites – three-lobed animals – were named by Johan Walch in 1771. Walch said they were molluscs, but over the years their affinities had been disputed. The problem was that only the hard back armour of the creatures had ever been found. In 1808 a French savant, Pierre Latreille, offered a simple and precise solution to the problem: if it could be shown that the trilobites had no legs then they must have been molluscs; if they had legs then they were woodlice, he said.

Walcott was the first to find trilobites with legs and settled the matter definitively with a note he published on them in 1876. Subsequently he published notes on the eggs of the trilobite, on the injury one had sustained to its eye while moulting, and on the animal's capacity to roll up for protection – just like some modern woodlice. Walcott became an acknowledged authority on the subject, and his expertise soon earned him a position with the United States Geological Survey.

Nearly 30 years later, in 1907, Walcott became Secretary of the Smithsonian Institution in Washington DC. Now at last he had time to explore further afield the Cambrian sequences that had always been his first interest. In the autumn of 1909 he followed the trail that his brother-in-law, George Vaux, had blazed through the mountains flanking the Burgess Pass in the Canadian Rockies. Along the track that traverses the western slope of the ridge between Mount Wapta and Mount Field his horse stumbled and Walcott decided to take a short break. Sitting there on the narrow trail, he idly picked up a small block of dark shale that had tumbled from a cliff some distance above. He took his hammer and split the block, as geologists are apt to do as a matter of course, and to his considerable astonishment found within it the delicate fossil impressions of several soft-bodied marine animals. Quite by chance he had discovered what no one had thought would ever be found: the fossil evidence of creatures that bridged the gap between single-cell organisms and the main thread of life's story.

Thereafter the Burgess Pass and its fossil-bearing shales became an annual pilgrimage for Walcott and his family. From 1910 to 1917 they spent several months of each year there. Science was the reason for the expeditions, of course, but there is also an element of the idyllic in Walcott's accounts of their journeys along old Indian trails through the mountains and upland meadows. High up in the Rockies they occasionally encountered snow even in July, and there was always some in September, but while on the move their tents were simply canvas sheets stretched over an open frame of stripped spruce poles. From the base camp in the forest just below the ridge to the east of Mount Burgess there was a beautiful view of the Emerald Glacier. They kept another tent up at the quarry – no trees or shelter of any kind up there – and frequently stayed there overnight. The best fossils they found came from the bottom metre of the deposit and they had to use explosives to get at them.

The Burgess Shale deposit is more than 2,000 metres above sea level today; 550 million years ago it was a mudbank, 100 metres beneath the sea. The Earth's relentless workings have moved seabed to mountain top and in the process turned fine silt and mud to rock. Within the layers of this rock are preserved exquisite fossil images of life from a time when the Sun shone harshly from a sky unmellowed by atmosphere even at dawn and dusk.

To preserve the soft body tissue of the animals that lived all that time ago required very special conditions indeed. The Burgess Shale community occupied ledges on a steep undersea cliff. From time to time the mud would slip off the ledge and the entire community would be carried away into deep, cold, oxygenless water where the animals did not decay, but instead were slowly flattened in their complete and original form as the mud gradually compacted under the weight of yet more sediment falling from above. Twenty-five centimetres probably compressed and solidified to rather less than one centimetre of rock. The result of many underwater landslides was one metre of shales containing the wafer-thin images of life in the seas over 500 million years ago.

Buried in the Burgess Shale are creatures that bear no resemblance to anything ever seen anywhere else on Earth. One, a segmented swimmer that Walcott named *Opabinia*, has five compound eyes on short stalks on its head, and a long flexible trunk with spiked pincers at the tip which it used to catch its prey. Another, aptly named *Hallucigenia*, has seven pairs of stilt-like legs, and seven tentacles on its back. In one slab of rock, 15 of these creatures were found clustered around a large worm, as though gathered for a feast.

It is barely possible to imagine those muddy ledges 100 metres below the surface of the sea, 550 million years ago. There is life, but is it recognizable among these oddities that have no common names, nor even common existence except as specimens in museum cabinets? There are jellyfish, and there are sponges like the ones that Wilson cut up and squeezed through his muslin bag, and rising from the mud, quivering across the ledge, then burrowing into the mud again is a slim silvery creature, like a narrow leaf, about eight centimetres long. The front end has a small coronet of tentacles around an opening through which it sucks in water. There is nothing that could be called a head, only a small, light-sensitive spot that might evolve to be an eye; there are no fins or limbs . . . but there *is* something familiar about it. Like no other creature in those early seas, it undulates, sending a series of rhythmic waves down the length of its body; the waves push the water backwards and move the animal forwards. To do this it must have a series of muscles attached to a firm internal structure. This animal has a rudimentary backbone.

Walcott called this creature *Pikaia*. About 30 specimens are known in all, and the rudimentary backbone, which is called the notochord, is evident in most, while in some the transverse bands of muscle that powered the creature can be made out too. Across vast expanses of time and space, *Pikaia* stands at the very beginning of the vertebrate progression that ultimately produced mankind.

Overleaf: this surreal reconstruction of a scene on a sea floor of the Cambrian period shows creatures known only from the delicate fossils found in the Burgess Shale. The stilt-legged *Hallucigenia* (foreground), and the five-eyed *Opabinia* (centre) bear no resemblance to any living form; *Eldonia* (floating in background) is distantly related to the modern sea cucumbers; *Vauxia* (standing erect) was a sponge and the wispy *Marpolia* was a form of alga.

In the early 1800s a veritable revolution in thinking about the formation and age of the Earth was taking place. The science of geology was being founded. Among several important developments it had been recognized that the layers of rock found in cliffs and gorges could be identified by the distinctive fossils they contained, and could therefore be correlated from place to place. Thus the red sandstones of Devon were shown to be identical to those in Scotland – the layers contained similar fossils and therefore must have been laid down at roughly the same time. Now it was possible to divide the history of the Earth into a sequence of geological periods and to give an indication of their relative ages.

Until the 1830s the oldest known period was the Devonian, named after Devon, the region in which its characteristic red sandstones had first been studied. Then two good friends, Adam Sedgwick, former student of theology, and Roderick Murchison, former army officer, entered the field of geological investigation, and defining the Earth's most ancient rocks became something of a contest.

In 1835 Murchison found a formation of fossil-bearing rock in Wales that lay beneath the Devonian and was therefore much older. He called it the Silurian, after the Silures, an ancient tribe which had resisted the Roman invasion of Wales.

During the course of the following year, Sedgwick found another formation lying, he claimed, beneath Murchison's Silurian and there-fore even older. He called it the Cambrian, from Cambria, the ancient name of Wales itself.

Thereafter the two men travelled extensively through Britain and Europe, establishing wherever they could the borderline between the Silurian and the Cambrian. Increasingly, their interpretations tended to overlap. Often, Sedgwick's Cambrian would be Murchison's Silu-rian, and vice versa. Finally they became irreconcilable enemies, Murchison contending that there was no boundary at all between the formations; the Cambrian was merely a local aspect of his Lower Silurian, he claimed.

Sedgwick resisted vigorously but to little effect, especially once Murchison became Director of the British Geological Survey and pushed through a ruling that the name Cambrian should be deleted from all official maps and publications.

The antagonism persisted throughout their lives, and only after the two men had died (Murchison in 1871, Sedgwick a year later) did it become clear that Sedgwick had been right all along. The Cambrian is a highly important period of the Earth's history. The Burgess shales are from the Cambrian period. The Silurian as Murchison defined it, on the other hand, is no longer regarded as a complete unitary period. Geologists now generally refer to Muchison's Lower Silurian as the Ordovician (after another ancient British tribe) and to his Upper Silurian as simply the Silurian.

*   *   *

Marine invertebrates had increased dramatically in abundance and diversity by about 450 million years ago; horn corals, finger-like bryozoans, brachiopods, trilobites and snails (top) were common. The trilobites, the tentacled cephalopods (left), and the eight-legged sea scorpion (right) eventually became extinct, but their living relatives include the octopus, the squid and the horseshoe crab.

In late Ordovician and in Silurian times, about 400 to 450 million years ago, the land mass that is now the British Isles lay much closer to the equator than it does today; the same was true of North America. Tropical reefs fringed a seashore where Wenlock Edge is situated in Shropshire, England, and where the Niagara Falls make such a spectacular show in the United States. There were shallow seas with warm clear waters, ideal conditions that promoted the prolific growth of corals, algae and shellfish. Among the corals there were crinoids, looking like delicate sea lilies but actually animals with fronded heads waving from long stalks, and there were all sorts of trilobites, some so commonly found as fossils that they have been given local names. The 'Dudley locust' is often found rolled up, just like a woodlouse. The 'strawberry-headed' trilobite has eyes on stalks, and the 'bald-headed' trilobite is well known for its large compound eyes, remarkably well preserved and easily seen with a magnifying glass.

The shallow Silurian seas were host to a great variety of organisms, each ensconced in its particular niche, but here and there something entirely new was nuzzling its way across the sea floor and into the story of life. They were small creatures, never more than ten centimetres long, with a wiggling tail and a disproportionately large head. Usually only the heavy plate-like bones of the head were found preserved in the fossil beds, so at first they were thought to have been water beetles, or molluscs, a new trilobite perhaps, or even a kind of tortoise. That they might represent some kind of ancestral fish was hardly considered, but in fact these oddities from the Silurian period, the first-known expression of the vertebrate form since its appearance in *Pikaia*, opened one of the most important chapters in the story of life: the Age of Fishes.

At the close of the Silurian period 395 million years ago convulsions shook the Earth again. Volcanoes and earthquakes raised to the height of mountains regions that had formerly lain under the sea. This was the beginning of the Devonian period. The weathering and wearing down of the newly raised land-forms produced huge quantities of pebbles, sand and mud, which were deposited in inland basins, and in vast coastal deltas. These deposits compacted and solidified to become the Old Red Sandstone formations that are most notably developed in Scotland, in the Welsh borderland and in Devon.

In the early nineteenth century these deposits were exposed to the hammers, chisels and prying fingers of inquisitive men, and everywhere they found fossils; there were oddities among them, but they were predominantly fossils of fish. No wonder that the young Swiss expert on fossil fish, Louis Agassiz (1807–73), was invited to Britain in 1833 to examine the thousands of specimens in the museums and private collections.

Among the British fossil fishes were a number of the puzzling, disproportionately large armoured heads. A few still had the tail attached – 'like a crab in front and a mermaid behind', commented one zoologist of the day. One specimen in particular, beautifully preserved in a small slab of Old Red Sandstone from Lower Devonian strata exposed at Glamis in Scotland, had a heavily muscled tail, fringed with fins, extending from the large, armoured, box-like head. It was about the size of a minnow, the ribs were visible, and even the individual vertebrae of its backbone could be made out. Agassiz named the specimen *Cephalaspis lyelli*, in honour of Charles Lyell (a founding father of geology), and he was so certain of its piscine affinities that he classified it and all the other puzzling armoured heads as fish. Subsequently they were acknowledged to be a distinct group of primitive fish and given the name ostracoderm, meaning bony shield.

The strong flexible backbone makes the ostracoderms the first known true vertebrates, but they were very primitive fish indeed. Their tail could propel them forward, but they had no fins capable of lifting them from the sea floor and therefore they could not swim in true, fish-like fashion. The heavy heads weighed the ostracoderms down and kept them nuzzling along the bottom, where they scooped in mud and sand through a simple circular mouth, filtered out edible scraps and expelled the remainder through slits on either side of their heads. They did not have jaws.

One hundred million years stretch between the rudimentary backbone of *Pikaia* in the Burgess Shale and the firm backbone of the ostracoderms in the Devonian, and absolutely nothing is known of what happened in between. No fossils have been found with evidence of any intermediate stages. Like so much of the story of life on Earth, it is as though the progression is a series of giant leaps from landing to landing up a stairway that has no steps; like mankind's journey to the moon, perhaps. If you take away all the words and pictures recording that giant step, what hard evidence is left? Just a few footprints.

Nevertheless, having arrived, the ostracoderms flourished. For 60 million years, from 410 to 350 million years ago, these primitive fish exploited their aquatic niche. They multiplied, and diversified into a variety of different species; then, almost as suddenly as they had entered the story of life, they disappeared from it, leaving only their fossil remains in the rocks as evidence of their existence, and today's parasitic lamprey and the scavenging hagfish as their sole descendants and inheritors of their once revolutionary lifestyle.

The most probable reason for the sudden disappearance of the jawless primitive fish was the development from among their kind of a creature with jaws that acquired the habit of eating them. Sixty million years in the same ecological niche does two things to a species: firstly, creatures become set in their ways and less capable of adapting to changes in environmental circumstance; secondly, the continuous exploitation of one niche sets a premium on the discovery of another. At some stage of the ostracoderms' existence, the reshuffling of the genetic code that occurs with every generation threw up variations in the structure of the head that bestowed survival advantages upon the individuals possessing them. Progressively, this interplay of genetic variation and survival advantage produced a fish with jaws. And just as the jawless fishes had multiplied and diversified dramatically, so the advent of the jaw set off an explosion in the number and variety of

Overleaf: the advent of the jawed fish consigned most of their jawless ancestors to extinction, although some have been preserved as fossils (top), while their descendants (below) still populate the oceans. Three hypothetical stages in the evolution of the jawed fishes from their jawless ancestors are shown in the central diagrams. From top to bottom: the third gill arch (white) is transformed into a jaw, while the fourth (blue) becomes a supporting structure. Teeth evolved from scales around the mouth. The skeleton (yellow) strengthened, and this, combined with the development of paired fins (red outline), brought greater speed and manoeuvrability, to be co-ordinated through the nervous system (spinal cord shown in magenta).

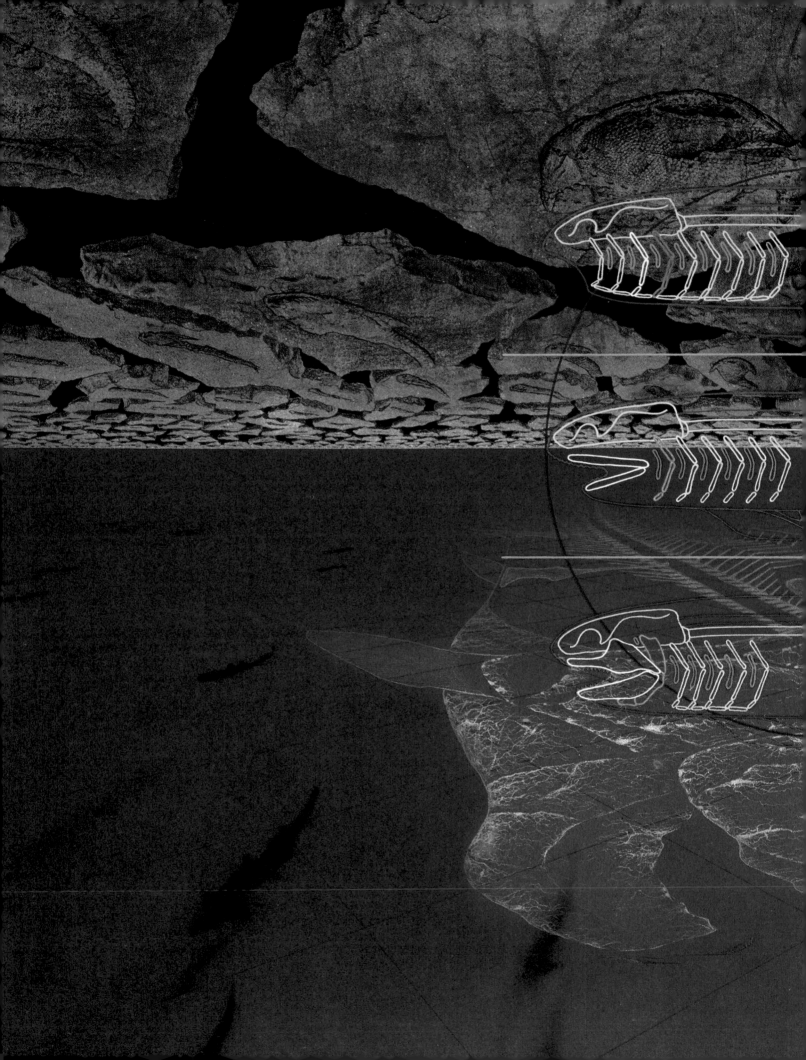

jawed fishes – largely at the expense of their jawless antecedents, who became a prime source of food.

Again, there is no fossil evidence of the developmental stages that came between the jawless and the jawed fish, but that is not altogether surprising. Only a minute fraction of the creatures alive at any one time die in the very special conditions that will lead to their preservation as fossils, thus Silurian and Devonian fossil fish are plentiful only because there were millions and millions of them alive during those millions of years. By the very nature of things, the progressive changes in head structure that bestowed survival advantage and eventually produced the jaw would only have been present in a very small number of individuals to begin with, and the evidence of their existence is likely to turn up in the fossil record only when there are enough of them to be numerically significant. Given that the fossil record compresses millions of years into a few metres of rock, the gradual increase of the living creatures to significant numbers over a very long period of time is inevitably reduced to an apparently sudden arrival of their fossil remains in the sequence.

*   *   *

In the north west of Australia, near a place that the Aborigines call Gogo, some strange cliffs rise over 300 metres high from the dry ranch lands of a cattle station. The cliffs are composed of ancient coral. Today they face an arid land dotted with dense masses of porcupine grass and the odd stunted mulga tree; 400 million years ago they were reefs along the borders of lagoons. The sea was here then, and rivers flowed into it from the land behind the reefs. When the rains were heavy inland the rivers were laden with mud which periodically stifled the lagoons with sediment, killing fish and trapping their corpses in the muddy sands that settled on the bottom of the lagoons.

Sometime later the lagoons filled entirely, the sea retreated, the Earth convulsed and in a period of worldwide continental upheaval, Australia rose above the waters. Now rain and rivers began to erode the sandstone that had filled the lagoons. The process continued for millions of years, eventually leaving the ancient coral reefs – much harder rock – standing alone.

The natural events that created the Gogo landscape are easily summarized, but defining the nature and origin of its curious features was a much more difficult task. Months of field survey and laboratory analysis were involved, but in the end there was an unexpected bonus. Strewn across the land at the base of the ancient coral cliffs, on what was once the ocean floor, geologists found among the dunes and scrubby bush a profusion of curious nodules. Someone took a hammer, broke one open and found a beautifully preserved fossil fish inside. Subsequently the team took large numbers of these nodules back to the laboratory and soaked them for several months in baths of

The evolution of the jaw brought a new predatory twist to the story of life. *Dinichthyes* (above left) and *Climatius* (below) were two of the many killers that lived in the seas of Devonian times.

acetic acid. Gradually the exterior stone crumbled and fell away, revealing a startling array of complete fossil fish.

Apparently, the fish that died in the lagoons nearly 400 million years ago had acted as catalysts when the muddy sea floor turned to rock; as they fossilized the mud and sand around them became particularly hard, resisting erosion while the rest of the sandstone deposit crumbled away. But the interesting thing was that these were fossils of placoderms, the world's earliest true fish, the jawed killers that replaced the jawless ostracoderms in the story of life. The placoderms (or 'plate-skinned' fish) gained their ascendency during the early part of the Devonian period. Their fossil remains have been found in many places, but the Gogo collection is unique in its variety and detail.

The placoderms represent the arrival of the vertebrate killer in the story of life on Earth. There were many different species and they came in all sizes: some were gigantic – up to nearly ten metres long. Like their jawless antecedents, most were armoured in some way, with heavy scales attached to bony plates in the skin, and they all had well-developed lateral fins, usually in two pairs: pectoral fins just behind the head and pelvic fins at the rear, as in modern fish. Although some species hugged the sea floor, the placoderms were accomplished swimmers. Guided by sight, propelled by muscles pulling on a strong internal skeleton, steered by paired fins, armed with jaws and a formidable array of teeth, the entire ocean was their niche, and any creature their prey. Confronted with such predators, virtually all the jawless fish species soon dwindled to extinction.

One could speculate long and hard on the evolution of the jaw, the tooth, the gills, the eye and the fin, but the significance here is that after nearly three billion years of life on Earth, this combination of features in the placoderms set the stage for the most spectacular and prolific radiation of forms. This is the point from which sprang all the diverse vertebrates: the amphibians, the reptiles, the birds and the mammals, not to mention the fishes themselves. Today more than 21,000 different species of fish are known, which is more than all other vertebrate species combined.

While the placoderms were ruling the oceans, the water's edge still marked the limit for life on Earth. An oxygen-rich atmosphere now enveloped the planet; rain fell and scoured its way to the seas; lakes and swamps filled land depressions – there was no shortage of aquatic environments and so far nothing had ventured into the terrestrial environments. The move was inevitable, however, and the plants were the first to break the barrier, beginning with algal patches at the water's edge. Then reed-like plants evolved and spread further from the water. Bushes and trees evolved from the reeds and by the end of the Devonian period, 345 million years ago, forests covered a good deal of the land surface – very strange looking forests, with trees standing high on exposed branching roots, their stems as scaly as a reptile's skin. Insects evolved from among the aquatic invertebrates and followed the vegetation ashore, but for a long time the vertebrates remained on the other side of the water's edge.

The paired fins of the Devonian fish were the anatomical forerunners of the vertebrates' paired limbs. *Eusthenopteron* (bottom) was one of a group of fish that could probably 'walk' on their lobe-like fins. *Ichthyostega* (above) was one of the first amphibians, a group that was equally at home in water and on land.

Overleaf: the climatic changes of the Devonian period probably determined the vertebrates' move from an aquatic to a terrestrial environment. While countless species became extinct, muscular fins and the ability to breathe air enabled fish such as *Eusthenopteron* to survive on land long enough to crawl from pool to pool as lakes and rivers dried up.

One might imagine that among the vertebrates flourishing in the oceans some species must have perceived the advantages awaiting any that managed to find their way ashore. It seems hardly credible that such a wealth of vegetation, standing ready to feed the adventurous, would not have attracted the vertebrates ashore. But two important factors rendered such a move improbable. Firstly, the aquatic vertebrates did not have the physical equipment – legs, teeth, digestive organs and so forth – that would have enabled them to reach and eat land plants, and secondly, it is extremely unlikely that they possessed any mental faculty remotely resembling a sense of perception. Their lives were entirely directed by the instinctive responses that had evolved over many generations to suit their immediate environment. They were programmed to live under a particular set of circumstances and, for the most part, could not survive in any other – much less perceive and take advantage of alternative opportunities. So the line of aquatic vertebrates from which the land-dwelling species evolved could not have been drawn from the water by the attractions of the terrestrial environment. On the contrary, they were stranded on the shore and managed to survive there when the climate changed and their aquatic environment shrank dramatically. Many aquatic species became extinct when this happened, but some possessed certain physical characteristics enabling them to adapt to the changing environment, and these species eventually became the ancestors of the terrestrial vertebrates.

As the Devonian drew to a close the Earth's climate became more extreme. Violent rains alternated with intense droughts. Oceans receded. Vast expanses of the continents turned to desert, and as drought tightened its grip, rivers ceased to flow; strings of ponds that marked the watercourses turned steadily to mud and finally dried rock hard. Around the world lakes and rivers dried out completely, trapping millions of fish (and thus creating many rich fossil deposits) as their aquatic environments turned terrestrial.

Numerous species of fish must have migrated from salt to fresh waters as the Age of Fishes progressed, but those doing so as drought became commonplace in the late Devonian must often have found themselves in water appreciably warmer than the sea they left behind. The shallow waters of lagoons, estuaries, rivers and lakes warm up rapidly. As water becomes warmer its oxygen content is reduced, making it difficult for fish to breathe. Many suffocate, but among the early colonizers of the shallow warm waters some fish developed the trick of gulping air from the surface and holding it in the gullet, where fine blood vessels absorbed the oxygen direct. With the passage of time and countless generations, this system of air-breathing evolved to find its most lasting expression in the lungfish, which could survive in oxygen-depleted waters while gill-breathing fish died in their thousands. To stay alive the lungfish needed only to rise to the surface of the water for air. Later it developed nostrils, which further facilitated inhalation, and it even acquired the habit of retiring into the mud as watercourses dried up, waiting there in a state of aestivation (a hot weather version of hibernation) until the next rains washed them out again.

While the evolutionary process was leading the lungfish towards aestivation as a means of surviving drought, it was also refining an alternative answer to the same environmental problem in another group of fish. The alternative answer was mobility. Instead of sitting out the drought, the fish in question would retreat from it, across dry land if need be, and it was this strategic response to the problems of drought that finally endowed the vertebrates with the means of moving from the water to the land.

The strategy evolved in a group known as the lobe-finned fish. The basic equipment they employed was common to all the placoderms' descendants: two pairs of fins, one pair just behind the head and another near the tail. But the lobefins were powered with a greater mass of muscle than their cousins, and their fins were longer, stronger, and constructed in a way that was quite new. Where the fin joined the body a single bone formed a 'shoulder' joint with the main skeleton; in the next part of the fin there were two bones, and finally there was an irregular branching of small bones.

The limbs that have carried the vertebrates through the story of life evolved from the fins of the lobe-finned fishes. The basic structure of shoulder, elbow and wrist, and hip, knee and ankle, was already present in the fish that lived 350 million years ago, although its initial significance lay only in enabling the lobefins to support their own weight and to waddle from pond to pond down the riverbed and between lakes as the drought advanced. This also of course gave them access to the food that the terrestrial environment had on offer – a vast unexploited niche. The lobefins could already breathe air out of water; once they had evolved fins capable of lifting their bellies off the ground they were poised to lead the vertebrates' invasion of the land.

Chapter Four

THE MOVE ASHORE

colonizing a barren landscape

The Welsh naturalist Edward Lhwyd published the first edition of his *Lithophylacii Britannici Ichnographia* (A Picture Book of British Preserved Rock) in 1699, featuring many fossils from the Coal Measures, where much evidence of the Earth's early vegetation is preserved. Lhwyd could not explain exactly how fossils were formed but considered they were freaks of nature – accidentally made by natural processes.

Let us go back in time – just a few hundred million years. The lobe-finned fishes were indeed the precursors of vertebrate life on land, but they could never have established themselves there without some food – in the form of plants and insects. By the end of the Devonian period, about 345 million years ago, the plants and insects were well ensconced in a large number of the environmental niches that the Earth had to offer; a profuse variety of forms and lifestyles already existed among them on land. But how had they got there in the first place? And where exactly was the land they were occupying?

We view the ocean as a very foreign place – deep, dark and frighteningly unfamiliar. It may have been the home of our ancestors, but they are much too distant to evoke any fellow feeling that might break down the emotional distinction we make between land and water. But in fact the distinction between the two is a very tenuous one, fragile and short-lived.

Our bodies are 80 per cent water, a saline solution runs through our veins . . . and the globe is covered far more by ocean than by land. If the Earth's surface were absolutely smooth it would all be 2½ kilometres under water. Terrestrial life exists because the Earth's internal machinations have pushed a few bumps and plateaux in its crust above the surface of the water. And while life was evolving in the oceans, and continues to evolve there towards a future we can hardly glimpse, the bumps and plateaux have been experiencing a kind of evolution too. They have coursed about the globe like the rainbow swirls that glide across the surface of soap bubbles. They have sunk to the ocean floor, and have been buried close to the Earth's red-hot core; they have been fused by heat, raised up, joined together, broken apart.

Everyone at some time or another has been struck by the matching Atlantic coastlines of Africa and South America. Six hundred million years ago the continents actually lay next to each other on their sides, South America to the north, Africa to the south, their Atlantic coasts roughly in line with the equator. North America lay to the east. Antarctica, India and Australia were tucked in under what is now the east coast of Africa; China and Siberia lay further to the south west. The Earth's landmasses were joined together as a supercontinent straddled diagonally across the equator, centred on what is now the Atlantic basin.

One hundred million years later the supercontinent had rotated clockwise through nearly 90 degrees and some large chunks had, as it were, spun off. Africa was still at the core of the largest block, though upside-down, with today's Mediterranean coast very close to the South Pole. South America, Antarctica, India and Australia were still joined to Africa, but China and Siberia were quite separate landmasses lying along the equator to the west, while North America was another separate equatorial landmass to the east.

The continental drifting continued. Four hundred million years ago Africa lay with its centre at the South Pole, still joined to South America, Antarctica, India and Australia. North America was drifting in from the north, Siberia and China from the north east. The landmasses collided, raising mountains; they parted, forming oceans. Three hundred and fifty million years ago there were two grand continents again – one comprising North America, Europe and the USSR joined in about their present configuration, extending north-east from the equator, and the other continent centred around Africa at the South Pole.

The two continents joined yet again as one supercontinent about 200 million years ago, then they parted and drifted towards their present position. The trend will continue, and in another 200 million years the continents will probably be back together again.

The science that describes the fantastic global wanderings of the continents is called plate tectonics. It could be said to have begun in 1912 when a German meteorologist, Alfred Wegener, proposed a theory that at the beginning of the Mesozoic era, 225 million years ago, the Earth's landmasses had been joined together in the form of a single supercontinent, which he called Pangaea, meaning 'all lands'.

Wegener backed his theory with a mass of geological evidence. He pointed out that Cambrian rocks in Scotland were identical to those found in Labrador, across the Atlantic. Similarly, there were geological formations in the Ivory Coast that matched others in Brazil, he said, and rocks in East Africa that were the same as others in Madagascar and India. Turning to the fossil evidence, he pointed out an extinct form of snail that had once crawled about in both Europe and North America. And then there was the matter of the coal formations known to exist in Antarctica: coal was laid down in tropical climes, therefore the Antarctic landmass must once have been in the tropics.

Wegener's theory gained some support, but it failed to convince the majority. What it lacked was an explanation of precisely how the continents were propelled over the face of the Earth. What force was behind them?

The answer was not forthcoming until the 1960s, when a Princeton University geologist, Harry Hess, realized that the recently identified mid-ocean ridges that girdle the world like random seams on a tennis ball were in fact a system of fissures emitting molten basalt from deep within the Earth. As it spread outwards from both sides of the ridge the basalt pushed the older material ahead of it, thereby widening the oceans and moving entire continents.

Mindful of what had befallen Wegener's continental drift theory, Hess published his ideas in a paper entitled, rather cautiously, 'An essay in geopoetry'. There is undoubtedly an element of the poetic in the slow-motion wanderings of continents about the globe, but poetry or not, by the 1980s the idea of sea-floor spreading and continental drift had become virtual fact. Strong supporting evidence had accumulated, particularly in the field of paleomagnetism, which studies the Earth's past magnetic activity.

It has long been known that the Earth's magnetic poles are not located at the geographic poles; nor are they stationary, but have wandered extensively about the globe. Furthermore, the magnetic polarity reverses from time to time, and has done so more than 150 times in the last 76 million years. All this information is found in the magnetic characteristics of iron oxides locked up in volcanic rocks. As lava solidifies its iron oxides are magnetized to the direction the north magnetic pole then holds, and they stay that way, even while the pole and the continents move. By plotting the polarity of rocks of identical age from different parts of the world, it is possible to pinpoint the position of the magnetic pole at a given time with some accuracy, and a sequence of rocks through time will trace the wanderings of the pole and the movements of the continents themselves.

Now it has also been established that the Earth's surface is composed of eight large plates and a dozen or so smaller ones that move about the globe, carrying continents, islands and oceans with them. The pace is slow, just a few centimetres a year, but it is continuous and relentless.

The configuration and location of the present-day continents is shown in these maps which tentatively trace the movements of the Earth's landmasses back to 600 million years ago – as described in the text on these pages.

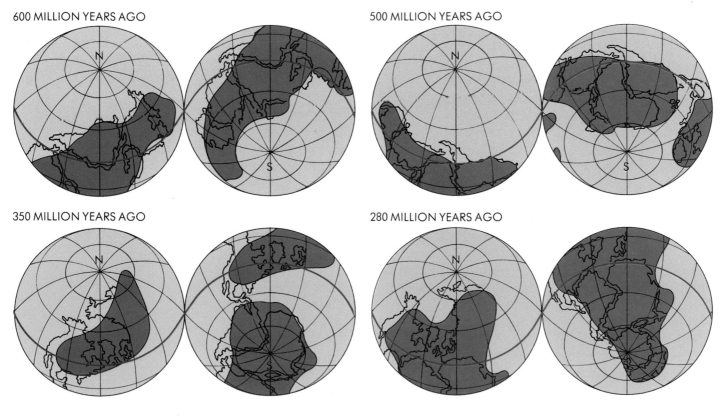

600 MILLION YEARS AGO

500 MILLION YEARS AGO

350 MILLION YEARS AGO

280 MILLION YEARS AGO

69

When plates collide one rides over the edge of the other, crumpling continents, raising sea floors, building mountains. Where two plates move apart there are fissures in the Earth's crust; where they grind alongside one another tremendous stresses are created – most of the world's earthquakes, volcanoes and great mountain ranges are found at the plate boundaries.

So plate tectonics and continental drift explain how it is that the fossil remains of sea-dwelling creatures are found over 5,000 metres up in the Himalayas and the Andes – the mountains were once part of the seabed – and why the British Isles show evidence of once experiencing an equatorial climate while Africa froze at the pole.

When life was confined to the oceans, none of these terrestrial upheavals would have had much more than a local, ephemeral effect on it. But when life spread to the land it was subject to the prevailing circumstances.

The environment confronting the first colonizers of the land as they evolved from the sea is commonly described as a desolate landscape of gushing volcanoes, dry barren plains, cruel desiccating winds and fierce sunshine. Undoubtedly such places did exist on the early Earth, and chemical-consuming prokaryote bacteria doubtless would have found their way there – washed ashore, blown on the wind. Their descendants are found there today, the bacteria that live on salts and on the rims of volcanoes. But no higher plants and animals have ever established themselves in these extreme environments, either now or at the earliest stages of life's terrestrial evolution. Nor have they needed to. There have always been better places available.

During the Silurian period, 430 to 395 million years ago, the climate around the world was generally mild, the continents had not yet been raised to any great heights, the seas were fairly shallow and plant life thrived in the waters. At this time the landmass of what is now the British Isles lay at the equator, most of it under water. Islands lay diagonally south-west to north-east from Ireland across the Irish Sea to Scotland. A long narrow stretch of land curved from the Atlantic across southern England and up to the Wash and the North Sea, bounded all round by shallow seas with coral reefs and a profusion of marine life. Viewed from the sea this coastline that is presently high and dry in the Welsh borderland probably looked much as the coast of northern Queensland does now on a fine day: an expanse of water, blue sky, clouds, sunshine; waves breaking on a coral reef; lagoons, whose vivid clear green shallows contrast sharply with the darker blue of the deep ocean beyond. At low tide clumps of green, red and brown seaweeds would have been exposed. There were extensive tidal flats and broad shallow deltas. The weather was relatively benign, warm and humid. Conditions such as these prevailed in many parts of the world – from what is now the USSR to the United States – and it was in such places that plant life first ventured ashore.

The land offered many advantages. Both the light and the carbon dioxide needed for photosynthesis were more readily available, and the land was unoccupied by competing forms of life. But even under relatively favourable circumstances the move from an aquatic to a terrestrial environment called for some fairly major evolutionary adaptations. There was the matter of support, for instance; in the water even the most flaccid plants were held aloft by internal air, but on land they would simply collapse. The embracing water also brought nutrients directly to a plant, and carried away the reproductive spores; there was no service like that on land, only the sun and air which would eventually suck all the moisture from any aquatic plant.

Initially, therefore, the first land plants would have occupied an in-between zone, perhaps on land regularly exposed by the departing tide. Here they gradually evolved the adaptations needed to survive in the air, while regular inundation allowed them access to the services of the sea. A waxy covering, a cuticle to prevent drying-out, might have been the first adaptation, possibly in a small, flat, photosynthesizing seaweed fixed to the shore at the edge of the tidal zone. The cells that held it in place developed into roots capable of seeking out nutrients. While the rise and fall of the tides still brought water to the plant as the medium for the dispersal of reproductive spores, rain occasionally performed the same function. A drop in ocean levels, a drying lagoon, left the pioneers stranded. A fortuitous round of rain showers helped them to survive. With the development of the cuticle to ward off desiccation, small openings were needed to permit and regulate the exchange of gases between the plant and the air around it – thus the stomata evolved. Now that water and minerals could only be absorbed through the proto-roots, instead of through the plant's entire surface, some kind of conduit was needed to carry these, and the products of photosynthesis, to the growing parts of the plant. As this conduit system evolved – in the form of the xylem to carry water and minerals, and the phloem for photosynthesized sugars – the plants' structure took on a form that was more efficiently adapted to its function: the stem evolved, holding aloft branches with the reproductive organs at their ends. These were the first vascular plants. The earliest known is called *Cooksonia*, it stood about six centimetres tall and was well established along the shores of equatorial Britain about 410 million years ago.

Not too long after *Cooksonia*, certainly by the beginning of the Devonian period 395 million years ago, the vascular plants had evolved into a dozen or so distinct species. Some of these were destined for extinction, but others were the beginning of the two major evolutionary lines from which has come all the world's vegetation. One was *Zosterophyllum*, a creeping rhizome-rooted plant with thin branched stems, about 20 centimetres tall, from which the clubmosses have evolved; the other was *Rhynia*, slender as a reed, about 17 centimetres tall, from which have come the ferns, the horsetails and the seed plants.

The primitive plants grew in dense clusters around the water-margins of the early continents. Deltas, coastal flats, river and stream banks were all soon colonized. Competition for light and space favoured greater height and a larger photosynthesizing surface.

Overleaf: terrestrial plants were well established by the time *Ichthyostega* (left) and *Eusthenopteron* found their way ashore. The rhizome-rooted *Protolepidodendron* provided varying degrees of ground cover, while ferns such as *Eospermatopteris*, the giant clubmoss *Archeosigillaria* and the luxuriant *Callixylon* soared to the height of modern trees.

Simple, spiny leaves appeared on *Asteroxylon*, a relative of *Zosterophyllum*, while the descendants of *Rhynia* became taller and more branched.

As the roots of the living plants pried into and broke apart their growing medium in search of nutrients, bacteria moved in and hastened the decay of dead matter and the first true fertile soils began to form. The plants were now firmly established on land; they were poised to colonize every available square metre, but their expansion was restricted by one very important factor – the need of water to assist their reproductive process. The terrestrial plants were still not entirely free of their aquatic ancestry.

Reproduction in primitive plants begins when the adult plant (the sporophyte) releases millions of asexual spores, all genetically identical to the parent plant. Spores falling on suitably moist surfaces grow into tiny matchstick-like plants called gametophytes, each of which sports both male and female organs. The male part matures first (a safeguard against self-fertilization) and releases microscopic male cells which must quite literally swim through surface moisture to seek out the female part of another gametophyte, which will have matured by the time they arrive. The fertilized female parts then grow into a new generation of adult plants.

This complicated procedure was all very well for the ancestral algae in the ocean, but it was a severe drawback for plants colonizing the land. Indeed, some plants never have escaped from their confinement to moist places; the direct descendants of the earliest plants, the clubmosses, ferns and horsetails, are still found there today. In time, however, a family of plants evolved with an innovative device that freed them to colonize drier parts of the terrestrial environment. The device was the seed, and the plants were the gymnosperms, which means simply 'naked seed'. This group includes the modern conifers, cycads and maidenhair trees.

The first seeds arose about 350 million years ago. Their evolution was an adaptation of the ancestral sporophyte–gametophyte process. In effect (and much simplified) the spores matured and became sexually distinct in the parent plant. Female spores grew larger and were retained in an ovule, where they were fertilized by the much smaller male spores that were released on the wind as clouds of pollen. The seed developed in the ovule; it became a hard viable entity capable of growing into an adult plant wherever and whenever it encountered a suitable growing medium.

During the period that lasted from 345 to 270 million years ago, when the continents were two large landmasses and the climate over most of the land was subtropical, warm and moist all year round, plant growth was phenomenal. Huge dense forests of remarkable uniformity covered the low swampy lands. Ferns, clubmosses, horsetails and the new seed-bearers grew into trees up to 45 metres high, with leaves one metre long. Eventually, because the trees were shallow-rooted and grew so close together, their debris began to exceed their rate of decay. The swamps became bogs. The land surface subsided, flooding the bogs with silty waters that ultimately buried the undecayed vegetation. This was the first stage in the making of coal.

The process continued for millions of years, laying down the major coal seams of the world. It ceased when the continents moved and climates changed some 270 million years ago; then the swamps dried up, the giant plants died out, and the geological period that is now called the Carboniferous came to an end.

*   *   *

Coal is fossilized fuel. What burns are the tiny fractions of the sun's energy preserved from when the ancient photosynthesizers had finished fuelling their own life processes and died. The energy was locked away in the carbon compounds of which the plants were composed; it was buried quickly under the silts, well away from the attention of bacteria, who would otherwise have used it to fuel their own lives. Then it was compressed, concentrated, and trapped within the crust of the Earth. Solar energy, fossilized in the remains of plants that lived hundreds of millions of years ago, now available to fuel other lives – indeed, it fuels an entire civilization.

The use of coal probably began in the Bronze Age, three to four thousand years ago, but it did not really get under way until centuries later when the lack of fuel wood became pressing. Fuel was always the primary motive for digging coal, but in pre-industrial times the activity brought the wealthy and educated more than just the means of warming their bottoms as they pontificated in front of the drawing-room fireplace – it also brought them strange fossils to place upon the mantelpiece, to puzzle over in the study and to discuss at learned gatherings and in publications.

Fossil shells and bones were already known from many places, but the coal mines seemed to produce only plants – and some very strange plants at that. In the eighteenth century fossils of any kind were one of the great puzzles. They were called 'formed stones', an unambiguous description that acknowledged accurately enough that they were made of stone and had been formed in some way. But how, where, when and why had they been formed? The received wisdom of the day was principally religious, and for most people religion supplied a satisfactory answer: the formed stones were relics of the Deluge that Noah had managed to survive. Taking the observation a step further, the formed stones thus became convincing evidence that the Deluge had indeed occurred – so live by the word of God, the Church advised.

But for some the explanation had always been unsatisfactory; it denied rational observation. Leonardo da Vinci (1452–1519) noted that '. . . if you wish to say that it was the Deluge which carried these [fossil] shells hundreds of miles from the sea, that cannot have happened, since the Deluge was caused by rain, and rain naturally urges rivers on towards the sea, together with everything carried by them, and does not bear dead objects from the sea shores towards the mountains . . .'

The huge dense forests of the Carboniferous period, which have subsequently supplied the fuels of our industrial age, were inhabited by a diversity of creatures. *Megalocephalus*, for example (right), was an amphibian; *Paleothryis* (centre) was a reptile, one of the first vertebrates to be entirely independent of the water and thus able to exploit a rich variety of terrestrial habitats; while the cockroach (lower left) was a very early insect.

Edward Lhwyd (1660–1709), a Welshman who at the height of his career was considered the foremost naturalist in Europe, was also puzzled by the origin and provenance of the formed stones. Lhwyd was appointed custodian of the Ashmolean Museum at Oxford in 1690 and devoted a good deal of energy to building up the museum's collection of formed stones and minerals. In 1699 he published what amounts to the first-ever catalogue of such things (with finance and help from Isaac Newton and Samuel Pepys, among others). It was entitled *Lithophylacii Britannici Ichnographia* (A Picture Book of British Preserved Rock) and in an appendix Lhwyd discussed the origin of fossils at length, inclining to the view that they were *lusus naturae*, sports or freaks of nature, accidently made by natural processes.

Lhwyd found it difficult to explain how such great numbers and such a variety of fossils could have formed by accident in so many places – perhaps fish spawn and plant seeds had fallen down through the rocks and formed there, he ventured – but he was quite certain that the Deluge had nothing to do with it.

'Had they been owing to the Deluge,' he wrote, 'we should find leaves and branches of such plants as are natives of our own island much more plentifully than such unknown plants as we cannot parallel: whereas on the contrary ... the generality of these mineral leaves are clearly distinct from those of our British plants.'

Lhwyd addressed that particular part of the appendix to John Ray (1627–1705), another pioneering naturalist who, towards the end of a distinguished career devoted to the study of nature, summed up his opinion of fossils with just a touch of exasperation:

'... there is a phenomenon in Nature, which doth somewhat puzzle me to reconcile with the Prudence observable in all its Works, and seems strongly to prove that Nature doth sometimes *ludere* [amuse itself], and delineate Figures, for no other End, but for the Ornament of some Stones, and to entertain and gratify our Curiosity, or exercise our Wits; that is, those Elegant impressions of the Leaves of Plants upon Coal-Slate. . . .'

The enquiries of rational minds prevailed, however. Robert Hooke, who was the first to apply the microscope to the study of fossils and in 1665 noted the resemblance between the internal structures of living and fossil wood, had no doubt that fossils were the relics of life in past ages, and therefore a key to the Earth's history. In the *Discourse of Earthquakes*, written between 1686 and 1689 but published posthumously in 1705, he wrote:

'... men do generally too much slight and pass over without regard these records of antiquity which nature have [sic] left as monuments and hieroglyphick characters of preceding transactions ... but those characters are not to be counterfeited by all the craft in the world, nor can they be doubted to be, what they appear, by anyone that will impartially examine the true appearance of them: And tho' it must be granted, that it is very difficult to read them, and to raise a *Chronology* out of them, and to state the intervals of the times wherein such, or such catastrophes and mutations have happened; yet 'tis not impossible but that, by the help of those joined to other means and assistances of information, much may be done. . . .'

During the hundred years that followed publication of Hooke's words much was done. Fossils were collected, compared, analysed and described to the point that their organic origin became indisputable; questions of just how they were formed and why they were found deep in the Earth were brought into sharp focus.

In 1749 the French naturalist Georges de Buffon published his observation that the parallel strata of the Earth 'were not formed in an instant, but were gradually produced by successive sediments'. De Buffon recognized the effects of erosion and tacitly acknowledged that the Earth's history was immensely long. In 1785 James Hutton presented his concept of the Earth as a 'beautiful machine', powered by heat, constantly renewing itself with 'no vestige of a beginning – no prospect of an end'. William Smith, an English engineer and surveyor, conceived the notion that geological strata could be defined by the kinds of fossils found in them, and that the same succession of strata and fossils could be identified wherever the same rocks were found. In 1799 he drew a map of ascending British strata. Georges Cuvier (1769–1832) published extensive studies of fossil vertebrates from around the world; Louis Agassiz studied fossil fish; von Schlotheim, von Sternberg and Brongniart studied the fossil plants, then in 1809 Jean Baptiste Lamarck published his proposal that all forms of life had progressively developed through time by the acquisition of advantageous characteristics.

The evidence accumulated year by year, answering many questions but still mutely awaiting the new ideas that would unlock its secrets. A synthesis was needed, one that would make the connection between fossils and the living world, and between fossils and the ancient Earth, assembling these seemingly disparate elements in a manner that would explain the story of the Earth and the development of life on it.

In 1834 Charles Lyell brought many of the elements together in his *Principles of Geology*, a work which at a stroke virtually founded the sciences of both geology and paleontology. Lyell stressed the view that natural forces held the Earth in a state of constant change. Since change occurred very slowly, barely discernible in the span of a man's lifetime, the process must have been going on for a very long time.

Meanwhile, the young Charles Darwin travelled the world, taking Lyell's *Principles* along with him. He collected strange fossils in South America, and in the Galapagos wondered why the finches were so different from island to island, when they all obviously came from the same stock. Similar questions occurred to Alfred Wallace during eight years spent collecting plant and animal specimens in the Malay archipelago.

Possibly the most significant key to the puzzle was an essay published by the Reverend Thomas Malthus in 1798. Malthus warned that human populations increasing unchecked would eventually run out of food and suffer dire consequences. From this Darwin deduced the relationship between population size and food supply and began to wonder about the mechanisms that kept population size under control. The potential for increase was enormous, even in the case of elephants, which breed slowly. Darwin calculated that with each generation surviving a normal lifespan, a single breeding pair of elephants could produce a standing population of 19 million individuals in 750 years. But in reality the elephant population remained essentially the same size.

Darwin came to the conclusion that a principle he called natural selection was at work, restricting population size to the carrying capacity of the environment, winnowing out some individuals and favouring others in terms of their reproductive success, and thereby effecting evolutionary change in the process.

Darwin's synthesis was published in 1859. Geological theory provided the timescale; the theory of evolution by natural selection described the process of change. Suddenly the fossils made sense and at once became an integral part of evolutionary theory. Together, fossils and theory are the basis of virtually everything that is known about the story of life on Earth.

There are times, however, when our knowledge rests rather more on theory than on hard fossil evidence. The origin and evolution of the insects is a case in point. Insects are the most successful creatures on Earth. Over 700,000 living species are known and there are probably a couple of million more awaiting discovery and description. They exist wherever there is something that can be turned into food, and even where there does not appear to be anything to eat at all, such as on the polar ice-caps and around hot volcanic springs; one species of fly manages to survive on the surface of natural crude oil ponds.

The success and diversity of the insects can be attributed simply to the adaptability of their basic structure – an external skeleton and a body divided into three articulating parts: the head with its two antennae, the thorax with its three pairs of legs, and the abdomen containing digestive and reproductive organs. All insects share these characteristics, although evolution has moulded them into a bewildering variety of forms, and adapted them to a large number of quite different lifestyles. If all living insects are basically the same, then the ancestral insects cannot have been very different. Tracing the origins and evolution of the insects through the fossil record should therefore be a relatively simple matter, but this is not so, mainly because the fossil record of the early insects can hardly be said to exist. There are a few scraps of fossil insect remains from about 350 million years ago, when plant life was just beginning to establish itself on land, but the next 50 million years of the insects' existence is entirely missing from the fossil record. Then, with dramatic suddenness, large numbers of them appear in the Carboniferous period. Fossils of all the major insect groups have been found from that time – cockroaches, grasshoppers,

Overleaf: an evocation of the Carboniferous period (345 to 270 million years ago). The giant dragonfly, portrayed life-size, has long been extinct, although the cockroach (on treetrunk and in ferns) is a common resident of the modern world, albeit on a smaller scale. Fossils show that the tassled horsetails (top right), finger-like clubmosses (bottom left) and ferns common in Carboniferous times were similar to living forms.

beetles, termites, dragonflies. . . . It is almost as though they had been delivered from another planet, ready-made. But their previous absence from the fossil record is more plausibly explained by the lack of the conditions required for preserving their remains on Earth than by their existence elsewhere in the universe.

Dead insects are delicate and not easily preserved. They are also a source of food for other insects and bacteria. The fossil record of life in the oceans is blessed with a large number of quite remarkable specimens, preserving details of the most delicate organisms. But these were buried quickly, perhaps while the creatures were still alive, by sudden falls of sediment from underwater cliffs, by shifting sands and muds. Patently, nothing like that occurred on land to trap the first terrestrial insects, or if it did it has yet to be found. So the fossil record of the insects really begins only in the Carboniferous, when swampy environments prevailed and there were sediments to trap and preserve a delicate dead insect here and there.

With few fossil clues to shed light on the history of the insects, the evolution of flight and metamorphosis, the divergence of the various groups, their arrival on land and above all their origin can only be deduced from the study of living insects and reference to evolutionary theory.

Fragmentary fossils around 350 million years old have been found in two locations, one a fossilized mid-Devonian peat bog discovered at Rhynie near Aberdeen in Scotland, the other an Upper Devonian deposit found in the USSR at Ukhta, to the north-east of Moscow. When it was discovered in 1961 the Ukhta specimen was believed to be a fragment of a wing, and its ancient owner was dubbed *Eopterum devonicum*, meaning 'dawn wing from the Devonian'. This suggested a very early date for the advent of flight, but debate on the matter was brought to an abrupt end in 1972 with the announcement that comparisons with other Devonian fossils had revealed that *Eopterum* was not part of a wing after all, but part of a crustacean tail fan.

The fossil peat bog at Rhynie was, of course, the home of *Rhynia*, *Asteroxylon* and other primitive plants that made up the Devonian flora. It was also, it seems, host to an active fauna as well. Puncture wounds on the fossil plant stems indicate that herbivorous insects had sucked the sap of the living plants, just as they do today; and the fossil remains of carnivorous springtails, mites and spiders have been found among the fossil plants.

All in all, the evidence from Rhynie clearly points to the existence of a well-integrated ecosystem 350 million years ago, with an established foodchain linking plants, herbivores, carnivores and presumably decomposers as well, and plenty of interaction between flora and fauna. Some microscopic fossil spores, for example, have hooks on them, which evolved either to deter consumers or to aid spore dispersal via the backs of consumers, but this only makes sense in the context of a long-established co-existing animal population.

The Rhynie animals themselves are already well advanced in evolutionary terms. Springtails, mites and spiders are specialized groups, classified along with the insects as arthropods (meaning jointed feet), but quite distinct from them, so the Rhynie creatures cannot have been the ancestors of the insects.

Prior to the Devonian there is only evidence of millipedes, and this poses as many questions as it answers. The oldest fossil millipede, found in 1899, comes from the Welsh borderland. The deposit is now known to be about 425 million years old, but over the years paleontologists have become less certain that the fossil represents the remains of a millipede. It is poorly preserved and has some affinities with fossil plant debris from the same site, suggesting that its origin may be floral rather than faunal.

Then there is the fossil that Thomas Huxley described (with Salter) in 1859. This too came from deposits now known to be over 400 million years old. It is a fragment of body case and leg, and was originally described as part of an amphibious crustacean. In 1899, however, the diagnosis was revised, and the specimen was held to be a millipede – a view that prevails among the majority today. But if the fragment did come from a millipede the whole creature must have been at least 275 millimetres long. And was it terrestrial? The specimen came from a filled-in channel deposit; it could have been washed down from some terrestrial location, but it might have been aquatic, or an amphibious version that regularly made the journey from ocean to land and back again. It is an open question.

Millipedes actually become quite plentiful in the fossil record of around 390 million years ago, both in the form of fossilized remains and in the trails they left on surfaces that were subsequently fossilized too. But this does not necessarily mean that they were the ancestors of the insects, or even that they were the only creatures around. It could equally well mean that theirs were the only remains to be preserved. The exoskeletons of millipedes are more durable than those of most insects, and perhaps the early forms moulted underground, as some modern millipedes do, where the shed skeleton was more likely to be preserved. And a millipede's trail through wet mud is much more likely to be preserved than any other evidence that an insect had been there – although it must be said that one authority has claimed to have found insect footprints on a specimen of fossilized land surface.

The authority in question was Anton Handlirsch, who was very active in the study of fossil insects in the first decades of the twentieth century. Handlirsch thought that the trilobites had been the ancestors of the insects; he suggested that their two lateral lobes had broadened and evolved into flapping organs as some among their number moved into shallow fresh waters and finally flew ashore as fully fledged insects.

At first glance the trilobites are fairly obvious candidates for the insects' ancestors. They were inhabitants of the oceans long before the plants moved ashore and, like the insects, they were made up of three sections, with a hard external skeleton, a pair of antennae and, in some cases, compound eyes. Handlirsch never abandoned his theory, but few of his colleagues ever agreed with him.

The trouble was that the trilobites were already a highly specialized group, clearly the product of a long evolutionary history. Such a degree of specialization is an unlikely starting point for the evolution of the more basic and general characteristics that the insects possess. Besides, the trilobites were a dead-end; the fossil record shows that they became extinct.

The only logical conclusion is that the ancestor of the insects in particular and the arthropods in general must have been a more primitive form. It was probably ancestral to the trilobites too, the lines having diverged way back in the early Cambrian, over 550 million years ago.

Although no fossil evidence exists of such an ancestor, the received wisdom of the 1980s suggests that it probably was something like the millipede. It would not have been difficult for an aquatic version to move ashore; legs and an external skeleton would have supported its body without the help of water, and the early stages of its evolution probably would have been amphibious, with ever-lengthening forays from water to land. The attractions of the terrestrial environment must have been considerable, nutritious plants and debris abounding, and who can say what problems the sea held that it was anxious to escape from? Doubtless marine selection pressure played a role in the matter, while the terrestrial environment offered a wholly unexploited niche.

The move ashore called for only two major adaptations in the ancestral millipede, the first of them concerning the most important matter of breathing. The aquatic form probably managed with something like the feathery gills on the inside of each leg that serve shrimps and lobsters today. But these would be useless out of water; they would dry out and stick together, thereby suffocating the creature. So the hypothetical ancestor must have evolved a network of breathing tubes that opened at the edge of each section of the shell and carried air to the various parts of the body, supplying each cell directly. This is how insects breathe today.

The second adaptation concerned reproduction, and this was more of a behavioural matter. In the ocean or pond the ancestor would have relied on water to ensure that sperm and eggs were brought together. In its amphibious stage reproduction would still have taken place in the water but eventually that constraint was broken too. Male and female got together, and the sperm was placed directly in the female.

Once the ancestral millipede was established ashore it was all set to evolve in any number of directions – it was just a matter of fusing its segments to form three parts; atrophying some legs, developing others; becoming larger or smaller. The process was mainly a mechanical response to changing conditions, but its climax must surely have been the development of wings.

Insects are the masters of flight, and have been for a long time. Even if the first flying insect took to the air only the day before the owner of the oldest-known fossil insect wing fell into the Carboniferous sediment, they have still been in the air about 150 million years longer than the birds.

The dragonflies are the first flying insects in the fossil record. They appear in deposits laid down about 300 million years ago, along with the many other insect types that suddenly seem to have evolved at that time. Some of the dragonflies subsequently became very large, with wingspans of over 700 millimetres. Insects resembling moths and butterflies are found in the deposits too, along with beetles and grasshoppers, so at least five different modes of flight had evolved by that time. But how had it all begun?

In the absence of any fossil evidence, theory and the example of living insects must suffice for an answer. There is a small living silverfish with a tiny flap extending from each side of the back of its thorax. Flaps similar to these could have developed into wings, although not necessarily for flight in the first instance. Insect wings carry blood through their veins, and so do the flaps on the back of the silverfish. Using them to catch the sunshine would have been a good way for the ancestral insect to warm up on cool mornings, and the development of muscles to move the flaps would have hastened the process.

Next, such an insect might have discovered that after climbing a plant to eat its spores or delicate leaftips it was much easier to leap off the edge of a leaf and glide to the ground (or to the next plant) on extended heat-transfer flaps than to climb laboriously down the stem. Many early plants had leaves cupped around the stem, which would have hindered descent and favoured an alternative method.

It can also be safely assumed that once the arthropods were established ashore they diverged rapidly, and even if the first flying insects were herbivores there were undoubtedly carnivores to eat them if they stayed on the ground. It could well be that the earliest flying insects were quite literally chased into the air by hungry spiders.

No matter how insect flight was achieved, its effect was far-reaching. During this time of relatively stable climate and heightened fecundity, competition for light and space produced ever larger and taller trees. As the trees climbed so did the insects. And as the insects became ever more adept at exploiting the vegetative food source – extracting sap, devouring leaves, spores, pollen and seeds – the vegetation evolved defensive responses, such as poisons and hard crusty shields. Some plants went a stage further and made a virtue of a vice: they used the pollen-eaters as pollinators.

Relying on the wind to carry pollen to the ovule was a very wasteful procedure, calling for clouds of pollen when only one grain was needed for the job. If an insect could be enticed to take the pollen direct it was welcome to all the pollen it could eat. Thus the flowering plants evolved – the angiosperms, meaning 'seed borne in a vessel'. Attracted by the colour, nectar and scent of a profusion of flowers, the exploiting insects were in turn exploited.

Chapter Five

═══ WHEN REPTILES RULED ═══

the time of the dinosaurs

The term dinosaur was used for the first time in Richard Owen's 1841 report on British fossil reptiles (top). Owen coined the term, meaning 'fearful lizard', to describe the group of large extinct reptiles whose fossil remains had been found by many collectors. The *Megalosaurus* and *Iguanodon* fossils (teeth, top) were found in the 1820s. *Scelidosaurus* (foot and limb bone) was described in 1861.

While the plants changed the face of the land, the vertebrates remained tied to the water for some time. By the mid-Devonian, about 370 million years ago, the lobe-finned fishes already possessed the equipment necessary for the move ashore. They could take oxygen direct from the atmosphere and sported fins with the bony structure of movable limbs strong enough to support their weight out of water. One of them left a trail through drying mud that became fossilized in the Old Red Sandstone deposits of the Orkney Islands – more a belly-scrape trough than a trail, in fact, with paddle-like depressions on either side – but there is no evidence in the fossil record to suggest that they ever managed to establish themselves in the terrestrial niche. They possessed the necessary equipment, but never made the behavioural adaptation. This was left to the amphibians, who were direct descendants of the lobe-finned fishes.

Richard Owen (1804–92), an early pioneer in the scientific study of fossils, made the first formal description of the earliest amphibians in his *Report on British Fossil Reptiles*, published in 1841. He dubbed them labyrinthodonts, meaning 'labyrinthine teeth', because their tooth enamel was so intricately folded that a tooth cut in section displayed all the complexity of a classic labyrinth in Crete. Most of the fossils that Owen described were heads: great flat, heavily built and spade-shaped heads with eye sockets and nostrils prominent on the top of the head, as though the creatures commonly floated just below the surface of the water with their eyes and nostrils protruding above it. There were jaws, too – with sharp tusks and fangs attached – and a number of vertebrae and limb bones.

Owen found anatomical features matching those of modern amphibians, and others that seemed to fall between the characteristics of fish on the one hand, and reptiles on the other. He described the ancient creatures as probably resembling gigantic salamanders, alligators and crocodiles, measuring anything from one or two to eight metres long. He thought it likely that a large labyrinthodont had been responsible for some curious fossil footprints which had recently attracted the attention of paleontologists. The fossil tracks in question, and the fossil labyrinthodonts, had come from similar deposits in Scotland; since neither quite resembled anything else, Owen felt confident in proposing that they were both relics of the same ancient creature.

Fossil tracks were something new in the early nineteenth century, and still the subject of dispute. The first ever recorded were found in the valley of the Connecticut River in 1802 by a local farm boy. They are now known to be the tracks of a small dinosaur, but the name dinosaur had yet to be invented then and the tracks were assumed to have been made by some ancient large birds. Folk of more biblical bent said they were probably the tracks of Noah's raven.

The tracks in Scotland, however, were not quite so simply dismissed. Found in 1828 by a clergyman, Henry Duncan, they were clearly the work of a large four-legged animal with a short stride and widespread feet – probably some sort of very large turtle, it was suggested. Professor William Buckland, a distinguished geologist of the day, decided to test this suggestion and invited a number of equally distinguished colleagues to observe the experiment. The idea was that some tortoises should be persuaded to walk across a bed of soft dough; the tracks they made would then be assessed and compared with those from the fossil tracks. But there were difficulties to be overcome, as a witness reported:

'. . . At first the beasts took it in their heads to be refractory and to stand still. Hereupon the ingenuity of the professor was called forth in order to make them move. This he endeavoured to do by applying sundry flips with his fingers upon their tails; devil a bit however would they stir; and no wonder, for on endeavouring to take them up it was found that they had stuck so fast to the piecrust as only to be removed with half a pound sticking to each foot. [It] was found necessary to employ a rolling pin, and to knead the paste afresh; nor did geological fingers disdain the culinary offices. It was really a glorious scene to behold all the philosophers, flour-besmeared, working away with tucked-up sleeves. Their exertions, I am happy to say, were at length crowned with success; a proper consistency of paste was attained, and the animals walked over the course in a very satisfactory manner; insomuch that many who came to scoff returned rather better disposed toward believing.'

The fossil tracks from Scotland had been made on land by a terrestrial animal of possibly amphibious characteristics, that much was clear. The fossil animals that Owen described bore several characteristics that were intermediate between the fishes and the reptiles – that too was clear. But even though the idea of evolving species was already moving strongly through the sciences, Owen did not draw the obvious conclusions because he firmly believed in the Creation. At the conclusion of his report on the fossil reptiles he took pains to refute any thought that the fossils he had described might support the suggestion that the characteristics of lower animals are progressively transmuted through time into the characteristics that distinguish related higher animals. He wrote:

. . . it is evident that many races of extinct reptiles have succeeded each other as inhabitants of the portion of the earth now forming

Great Britain; their abundant remains, through strata of immense thickness, show that they existed in great numbers, and probably for many successive generations. . . . To what natural or secondary cause, it may then be asked, can the successive genera and species of reptiles be attributed? Does the hypothesis of the transmutation of species, by a march of development occasioning a progressive ascent in the organic scale, afford any explanation of these surprising phenomena?'

Earlier in his report Owen had acknowledged the reptile-like anatomy of the labyrinthodonts, and did not deny that their dental structures resembled those of the lobe-finned fishes; he noted that fishes were the only vertebrates found in deposits older than those containing labyrinthodont fossils, but refused to make anything more of the fish-to-amphibian-to-reptile progression that he was in fact delineating. He found the gaps in the sequence more significant than the connections:

'. . . though a general progression may be discerned, the interruptions and faults, to use a geological phrase, negative the notion that the progression has been the result of self-developing energies adequate to a transmutation of specific characters; but, on the contrary, support the conclusion that the modifications . . . were originally impressed upon them at their creation, and have been neither derived from improvement of a lower, nor lost by progressive development into a higher type.'

Inevitably, however, once Darwin had published *The Origin of Species*, the labyrinthodonts were used to demonstrate the evolutionary progression of the vertebrates from fish to amphibian to reptile. But one very important, even puzzling, aspect of that transition was almost completely ignored for over 100 years, until the 1960s in fact, when the science of ecology came to the fore in the contemporary concern for the human environment.

Ecology describes the relationships and interdependences that exist between animals and their environment. One of its basic tenets has to do with what has been called the pyramid of life, which is related to the way energy is cycled and recycled through an ecosystem. It is quite simple: the sun's energy is trapped by photosynthesizing plants; plants are eaten by herbivores, which in turn are eaten by carnivores or omnivores, and the whole system is kept tidy by the decomposers, who break down dead material, thereby returning essential minerals and elements to the soil for use by plants in the next cycle. The key to the system is the amount of energy available at each level; this determines how large a population the ecosystem can support. Plants catch a given amount of the sun's energy by photosynthesis, but because they use most of it in their own life processes, only about ten per cent is available to build the herbivores that eat them; similarly, at the next level only about ten per cent of the energy consumed by herbivores is available to build carnivores. This means there can never be more carnivores than herbivores, and never more herbivores than plant life. The system forms a pyramid of life; the carnivores are at the apex, plants are the baseline. And the system is universal, it applies to all ecosystems, everywhere.

But at first glance the labyrinthodonts seem to contradict the principle. They were exclusively carnivorous, their fangs and tusks make that quite clear and there is no fossil evidence of a single herbivore among them. So although it is appealing to think of the terrestrial pioneers as large genial amphibians, lumbering ashore to find vast virgin pastures to browse through and wax fat upon, that cannot have been the case. The only thing for the labyrinthodonts to eat on land at that stage would have been insects – spiders, scorpions, millipedes and the like; hardly the diet to attract and sustain creatures weighing around 100 kilograms. It seems certain, therefore, that they must have been feeding in the water, still at the apex of an aquatic ecosystem, and were drawn to the land by some other motive.

Accounts of vertebrate evolution often tell how the move from water to land was restrained only by the early amphibians' reproductive procedures, which still demanded an aquatic environment. The story evokes the image of a pioneer glimpsing a new world, anxious to enjoy the unexploited resources it has found but held back by a tedious need to produce young in the water.

The reality is less dramatic: the large labyrinthodonts were tied to the water by their food requirements, and were probably quite content there. They were preceded ashore by much smaller amphibians, who consumed invertebrates in the water and made equally sustaining meals of the invertebrates they found in the course of exploratory forays on to the land. This probably occurred during the warm, humid Carboniferous period, when plant life and invertebrates were abundant on land and the waters swarmed with an impressive variety of large predacious carnivores, including the lobe-finned fishes and their labyrinthodont descendants. The little amphibians probably first ventured ashore seeking refuge from the aquatic predators, who followed only some millions of years later when the climate changed and seasonal droughts favoured the creatures that could waddle down to the next pool as the rivers and swamps dried out. It was this that brought the labyrinthodonts and their descendants ashore; they did not colonize the land directly, but were stranded there by the retreating waters, and managed to survive. Eventually, by the end of the Carboniferous, the terrestrial way of life prevailed. Amphibians of various sizes fed upon one another down to the smallest, which in turn fed upon the insects, worms and spiders that must have been plentiful in the forests. None of the vertebrates fed directly upon the abundant vegetation. They left the invertebrates to process it for them and, indeed, could never have survived on land if the invertebrates had not been there first.

Some time before the climatic crisis began to affect the amphibious lifestyle, the vertebrates went through a crucial stage in their evolution. Some among their number evolved the practice of producing their young neatly packaged inside a hard enclosing capsule: the egg.

During the Permian period (270 to 225 million years ago) numerous different forms arose among the early terrestrial reptiles, including the giant amphibian *Eryops* (foreground) and two mammal-like reptiles, *Cynognathus* (left) and *Dimetrodon* (right), whose spiny 'sail' may have helped to regulate body heat.

This wonderful miniature ancestral pond, in which the young could grow until they were old enough to fend for themselves, did not need to be anywhere near the water. The practice of laying eggs on dry land probably evolved while the coal forest swamps were still well watered, as a means of keeping the young away from predators, although it had other important benefits too. As the swamps dried out most of the amphibians died out, but the egg-layers among them were able to survive away from water, wherever there was some vegetation and some invertebrates to process it for them. These were the first vertebrate animals to live entirely on land – the first reptiles.

Once established ashore, the early terrestrial reptiles evolved rapidly. At first there was still a sizeable aquatic element in their diet and preying upon each other was common among the largest of them. Inevitably, however, some evolved the dental and digestive equipment needed to take advantage of the plant food that was at first so abundantly available. This development cut the last thread that tied the vertebrates to the water.

What followed next was a spectacular instance of what paleontologists have termed 'adaptive radiation'. Through the Permian period, between 270 and 225 million years ago, the early reptiles diverged at a rate that has hardly been matched before or since. Numerous species, genera, families and orders were established, and there were some remarkable specializations. *Dimetrodon*, for instance, carried a large 'sail' on its back, formed of elongated vertebral spines and probably something to do with the regulation of body heat. *Sphenacodon* had teeth like steak knives, flattened blades with serrated edges, capable of cutting up large prey into small pieces.

By the end of the Permian period large sections of the fauna were entirely free of the water. No longer entirely reptilian, they ruled the earth for 70 million years, evolving characteristics that would later lead to the evolution of the mammals; these creatures have been called the therapsids, the mammal-like reptiles. But before their evolution could proceed much further, they were nearly overwhelmed by another wave of reptilian adaptive radiation – dinosaurs, the 'fearfully great lizards', arrived on the Permian scene.

*　　*　　*

In 1677 Dr Robert Plot (1640–96), first custodian of the Ashmolean Museum, and Professor of Chemistry at Oxford, published a book called *The Natural History of Oxford-Shire* which included an illustration and description of part of a very large fossilized thigh-bone that had been given to him by 'the ingenious Sir Thomas Pennyston'. The bone, Plot wrote, had '... exactly the figure of the lowermost part of the thigh-bone of a man or at least of some other animal. ... In compass near the capita femoris [it measured] just two foot, and at the top above the sinus (where the thigh-bone is as small as anywhere) about 15 inches; in weight, though representing so short a part of the thighbone, almost 20 pounds . . . this stone . . . must have been a real bone, now petrified. . . . it must have belonged to some greater animal than either an ox or horse; and if so in probability it must have been the bone of some elephant, brought hither during the government of the Romans in Britain. . . .'

In fact Plot's illustration and description of the bone are the earliest known record of dinosaurs. During the next 200 years quantities of large strange bones were found and the images they evoked of huge and unimagined beasts caused more than just a stir of curiosity – they also galvanized the study of fossils into a science capable of adding substantive evidence to the study of life's development on Earth. In 1770, from the underground chalk quarries at Maestricht, came an enormous skull with dagger-like teeth set in jaws over a metre long. The creature was described as a 'monstrous monitor of the ancient deep . . . five and twenty feet in length'. Other notable remains came from workings near Paris, near Oxford and from the South Downs in Sussex. By the 1820s such finds were almost as valued as treasure trove, the sites jealously guarded in some cases and the fossils changing hands for large sums of money. One avid collector, Gideon Mantell, paid £25 in 1834 for some fossils from a quarry near Maidstone in Kent; and in 1839, when Mantell sold his entire collection to the British Museum, he received £4,000 from government funds.

Mantell's collection included the fossils he had found and described in 1825 as having belonged to a creature he named *Iguanodon*, a giant plant-eater resembling the living iguana lizards. Meanwhile, in 1822 James Parkinson, now remembered principally as the man who first described Parkinson's disease, gave the name *Megalosaurus* (meaning 'giant lizard') to the ancient owner of some large, serrated, blade-like teeth then in the possession of William Buckland. *Megalosaurus* was clearly a very large flesh-eating creature; Parkinson estimated its length at about 12 metres.

Iguanodon, Megalosaurus, Mosasaurus, Streptospondylus, Plesiosaurus, Ichthyosaurus, Teleosaurus, Steneosaurus, Poikiopleuron . . . the fossils, the names and their affinities proliferated greatly during this period, but they did not begin to tell a coherent story until the French anatomist Georges Cuvier established a method of studying the fossils systematically, and Richard Owen published his systematic study of the British fossil reptiles in 1841.

Cuvier introduced the principles of comparative anatomy that prevail to this day. He saw that all vertebrates are functional variations on one basic theme and showed how essentially identical structures are modified to suit particular ways of life – the bird's wing, the horse's foreleg and the human arm, for example. He noted that the form of certain anatomical parts is invariably related to the form of other parts: hoofs and horns always correlate with the large grinding molars of herbivores; claws are always associated with the fangs of carnivores. Thus Cuvier showed how individual skeletons could be sorted and assembled from a jumble of bones, and how creatures no one had ever

Under attack, the horned dinosaur, *Styracosaurus*, wheels to face the carnivorous *Daspletosaurus*.

seen could be reliably reconstructed from the evidence of a few fossil bones. Cuvier was the first to demonstrate the scientific fact of extinction.

On 2 August 1841, at the age of 38, Richard Owen stood for two and a half hours before the annual meeting of the British Association for the Advancement of Science, held that year at Plymouth, and delivered his masterly report on the British fossil reptiles. He had organized the fossils into a system of 59 species, 32 genera and nine orders. There were many new names among his descriptions, including the Dinosauria – the first public mention of the dinosaur concept which has so captivated the public imagination ever since. Equally significant was Owen's observation that the dinosaurs, despite their bulk, had walked efficiently with their legs directly under their bodies, unlike the amphibians with their widespread waddle. This assessment was based on the structure of the pelvis, which featured a ball-and-socket hip joint and brought the dinosaurs a much more effective means of getting about than had hitherto prevailed.

The dinosaurs, Owen concluded in his report, 'rejoicing in these undeniably most perfect modifications of the Reptilian type, attained the greatest bulk, and must have played the most conspicuous parts, in their respective characters as devourers of animals and feeders upon vegetables, that this earth has ever witnessed in oviparous [egg-laying] and cold-blooded creatures'.

In the following years many more dinosaurs were discovered in different parts of the world, but especially in North America where industrialists and the scions of wealthy families sank fortunes into what became a race to name new species. In the case of Professors Marsh and Cope the race began in 1872 and went on for 25 years; it became an ignominious affair that brought little credit to the memory of either man but did endow science with a superlative collection of dinosaur fossils.

In true Victorian spirit, Marsh and Cope collected with exhibition and display in mind. They went after the biggest and the best and the most startlingly different. The result was that with abundant dollars and the constant goad of a competitive rival, they probably identified most of the different species that were to be found in America, and sooner, more efficiently and with better prepared specimens than might otherwise have been the case.

Since the days of Marsh and Cope the full extent of the dinosaurs' success has been thoroughly documented. They dominated the Earth for about 140 million years, occupying the full range of environmental niches. By the 1980s more than 800 different species – large and small, insectivores, herbivores and carnivores – had been identified, but two questions remained unanswered: how had they achieved such spectacular success, and having become so successful why did they die out?

*　　*　　*

The herbivorous *Iguanodon* (right) was over nine metres long and weighed about four tonnes. The predacious *Deinonychus*, by contrast, was lightly built and agile; its tail was specially adapted to balance the animal at speed. *Deinonychus* possibly hunted in packs (left) – fearsome sickle-like claws on their hind feet were used to kill their victims.

Overleaf: the fossil remains of *Deinonychus* were found in 1964 in Lower Cretaceous deposits, about 100 million years old, at a site in Montana (upper left). The hooked claw (bottom), from which its name is derived (*Deinonychus* means 'terrible claw'), was a unique adaptation which, together with the ability to lock its tail rigid (top) while running, and its powerful jaw muscles (right), indicate a high level of activity, suggesting to some authorities that it may have been warm-blooded.

The therapsids – the mammal-like reptiles that preceded the dinosaurs in the story of life – ruled the Earth for a long time but they were essentially rather conservative. Having brought the vertebrate form ashore, they adopted a wholly terrestrial lifestyle and diverged into a large number of very different species, but their basic structure did not change much. In fact, the development of dental and digestive equipment that turned some of them into herbivores was their only really significant modification. They all retained the waddling four-footed gait, so none of them could move around especially well; none took to climbing trees or burrowing in the ground, none developed any offensive equipment other than teeth, and none had more than just a little defensive equipment either – no protective shells or plating. In short, the mammal-like reptiles rapidly acquired the few adaptations they needed to make a success of life on land and thereafter became just a little set in their ways. But their position was not as secure as it might seem.

At the waterside, the interface between two ecosystems that offers the riches of both to any creature that cares to exploit them, all had not stood still since the therapsids moved on. Evolutionary innovations had arisen among other branches of the reptiles' ancestral stock as well. In the semi-aquatic niche once occupied by members of the therapsid line there now lay, floating in the shallows, a creature that is known mostly from the evidence of its footprints. The first of these were found in 1834 in the Triassic red sandstones of central Germany, deposits that are now known to be between 225 and 190 million years old. The creature was named *Cheirotherium*, meaning 'hand animal', because a curiously angled digit on the outside of the print was thought to be some sort of thumb, and its owner therefore a bear, or possibly even an ape, even though only reptiles were known from such ancient deposits.

Forty years later it was proved that the tracks were definitely reptilian, and the subsequent discovery and analysis of more than 20 similar trails has revealed the full significance of the cheirotheres. The animal had strong claws, indicating a carnivorous way of life; the gait was predominantly bipedal and the body was about a metre long, balanced by a tail of similar length.

In the 1960s these tentative reconstructions, based on the evidence of footprints alone, were enhanced by the discovery and description of *Ticinosuchus*, an animal from the mid-Triassic formations of Switzerland. A bipedal carnivore with a stout muscled tail, slim hips and narrow gait, *Ticinosuchus* was soon rated prime candidate for originator of the cheirothere footprints, and not only that, for the origin of the dinosaurs as well. Perhaps it happened like this . . . .

While the early mammal-like reptiles colonized the land, the aquatic *Ticinosuchus* line moved up to the water's edge and became a four-footed carnivore that found rich pickings both on land and in the water, much as crocodiles do today. Like the crocodile it acquired a flatter and more powerful tail to propel it through the water after fish; and floating at the surface close to the water's edge it used its hind legs

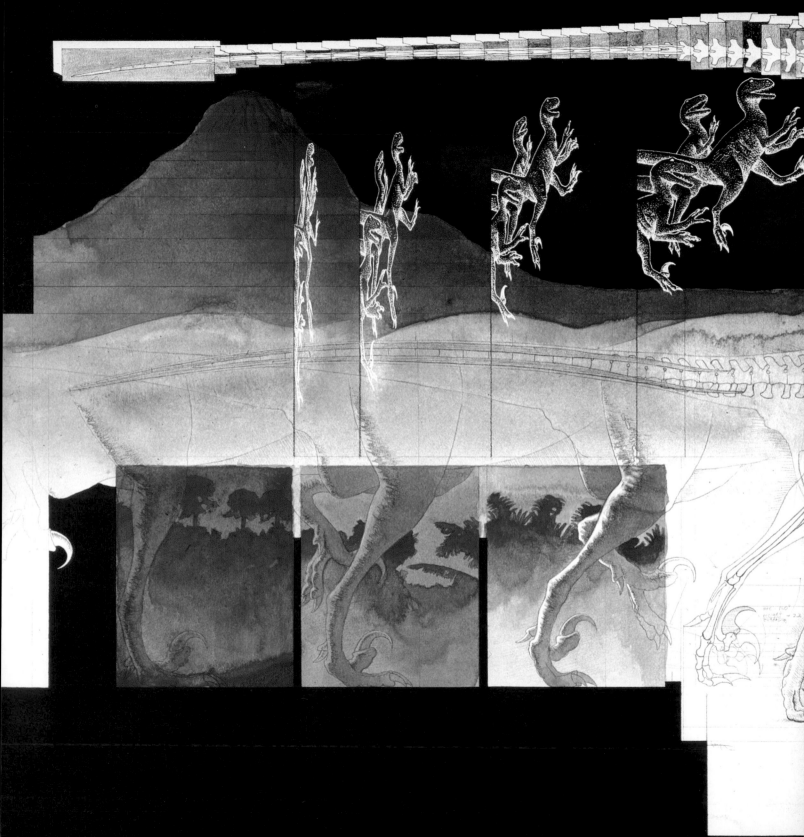

to leap forward and catch the unwary creatures that came down to drink. To be effective the leap forward had to be fast and powerful, the thrust of the hind legs had to be directed straight down beneath the body, not off to the side as in the waddle of the reptiles. The new strategy bestowed selection benefits on its most effective exponents. Adaptations arose. The pelvic girdle narrowed and fused and developed the ball and socket joint; hind limbs grew longer and stronger; forelimbs acquired the habit of grasping as well as swimming.

Telescoping 50 million years of evolution one might say that these ancestors of the dinosaurs ultimately walked on to the land with the legs to chase after, the hands to catch and the teeth to tear apart the mammal-like reptiles they found there. What is certain from the fossil record is that they took over. Beginning in the early Triassic period, about 225 million years ago, first the therapsid carnivores and then the herbivores were replaced by the ancestral dinosaurs. By 190 million years ago the mammal-like reptiles were just a thin line on the evolutionary map, all but overwhelmed by the great bulge of the dinosaurs' adaptive radiation.

The dinosaurs rapidly evolved to fill the available niches; insectivores, carnivores and herbivores, they were the largest land animals that have ever lived. Some were bipedal, others quadrupedal; some had horns, others were armour-plated, spiked, fanged, beaked, even duck-billed. Some returned to the water and flourished there; others took to the air.

The development of the flying dinosaurs began with the ancestral stock, and evolved in parallel with the dinosaurs, not from them, although bipedal gait was again crucial. Flight developed first in the shape of the pterosaurs (meaning 'winged lizards', although the creatures are also known as pterodactyls, meaning 'winged fingers') who in effect vastly extended the fourth finger of each 'hand', stretching a membrane from the side of the body to the fingertip, rather like huge bats.

The first pterosaurs appear in the fossil record of about 200 million years ago. Some 85 species have been described in all: some were the size of a sparrow, while others were larger than any other flying creatures ever known. *Quelzalcoatlus northropi*, for example, found in Texas during the 1970s, had a wingspan estimated at approaching 12 metres. The fossil evidence indicates that the pterosaurs included species that ate insects, and others that ate fish. One had teeth resembling the baleen grids with which blue whales strain plankton from the sea. Fossil skulls reveal the probability of well-developed eyes, and brain casts suggest a degree of cerebral specialization, and therefore muscular co-ordination, exceeding that which might have been expected of reptiles at that stage of their development. All in all the pterosaurs were a diverse and successful group. They were in the skies for 135 million years, so they can hardly be called a short-term experiment. Nonetheless, for all their success and longevity, extinction was their ultimate fate. They vanished from the face of the Earth some 65 million years ago.

100

The bat-like pterosaurs were a flying version of the dinosaurs. Among 85 known species some were the size of small modern birds, while others were the largest airborne creatures ever known – they had a wingspan of nearly 12 metres.

Birds evolved from the reptiles. *Archaeopteryx* (top) combined reptilian features such as teeth and foreclaws with the uniquely avian feature, feathers.

Overleaf: Archaeopteryx glides through the Jurassic forest of some 150 million years ago in pursuit of a lacewing insect, while in the background a dinosaur, *Diplodocus*, lumbers along through the trees (the sequoia-like *Taxodiacia*).

Happily, the other creatures of flight that developed along with the dinosaurs and the pterosaurs are still with us in spectacular and enchanting variety: the birds.

The first evidence of the earliest birds was found in 1861. It was a single flight feather, about 60 millimetres long, beautifully preserved in the fine-grained stone that was quarried at Solenhofen in Germany for use in the lithographic printing process. The feather was blackish, only the tip of the quill was missing, the fibres were clearly defined and even the tiny barbules on the fibres could be seen. There were impressions of the feather on both sides of the slab in which it had been found; it is not difficult to imagine how it had fallen into soft mud silts on the lake bed that had been the origin of those lithographic stone deposits. But the deposits were of Jurassic age, 140 million years old, and in 1861 no feathers or indeed any bird remains had been found in rocks older than the Tertiary period, which began a mere 65 million years ago. Birds appeared in the fossil record only after the extinction of the pterosaurs which, not unreasonably, were therefore thought to be the ancestors of the birds. The single feather seemed to turn this idea on its head, as the author of its initial description, Hermann von Meyer, fully realized.

In discussing the significance of the single feather, von Meyer drew attention to what he saw as the dangers of placing too much faith in Cuvier's theory that the similarity of parts must imply the similarity of the whole. The fossil feather may be exactly like those of modern birds, he said, but perhaps it had come from some other sort of feathered creature.

Within a month of acquiring the fossil feather von Meyer received word of another fossil, recently found in the same Solenhofen quarry, which might have been exactly what he had in mind. It was a creature about the size of a raven, with the skeleton and long tail of a reptile, but the feathers of a bird. Von Meyer described the fossil briefly, on the basis of information he received from two colleagues who had seen it personally, and named it *Archaeopteryx lithographica* – ancient feather of the lithographic stone. This fossil really set the cat among the pigeons.

1861 was just two years after Darwin's synthesis, *The Origin of Species*, had been published. *Archaeopteryx* seemed to be exactly the kind of fossil that the theory of evolution required as substantive proof – a creature that stood between two classes of higher animal while possessing some distinctive characteristics of both. The skeleton was reptilian, but the feathers were no different from those of modern birds, even though they grew from each vertebra down the entire

length of the tail, and not in a clump from the final vertebra as with modern birds. *Archaeopteryx* was, and indeed still is, *the* classic case of 'evolution caught in the act', a missing link, and the implications of this were not lost on the experts.

The German zoologist Andreas Wagner wrote of *Archaeopteryx* in a paper entitled *On a New Fossil Reptile Supposed To Be Furnished with Feathers*, first published in 1861. In it Wagner remarked that while the discovery of fossil feathers was itself unprecedented, the mode of their union with the skeleton bordered on the incredible. He added: 'Whether I regarded this mongrel creature as a bird with the tail of a reptile, or as a reptile with bird's feathers, was no matter; the one was as incomprehensible . . . as the other.'

Wagner came down finally on the side of the reptiles and, disregarding von Meyer's previous and quite valid attribution, named it *Griphosaurus* – the enigmatic lizard. But Wagner's true colours were revealed in the concluding remarks of his paper:

> 'At the first glance of the *Griphosaurus* we might certainly form a notion that we had before us an intermediate creature, engaged in the transition from the saurian to the bird. Darwin and his adherents will probably employ the new discovery as an exceedingly welcome occurrence for the justification of their strange views upon the transformation of animals. But in this they will be wrong. . . . I am entitled to ask of the Darwinians if they should decide to cite the *Griphosaurus* as an intermediate creature undergoing a transformation from reptile into a bird, to show me, first of all, the intermediate steps by which the transition of some . . . living or extinct animal from one class into another was effected. If they cannot do this (as they certainly cannot), their views must be at once rejected as fantastic dreams, with which the exact investigation of nature has nothing to do.'

Wagner adopted a bold stance but a significant weakness of his position was that he had not seen the fossil himself. In fact not many people had seen it at that stage, a state of affairs determined by the pecuniary ambitions of its owner, Dr Karl Friedrick Häberlein, district health officer of Pappenheim, just up the railway line from the quarries where the fossil had been found.

The quarrymen made a little money on the side by selling fossils. Dr Häberlein was a keen collector and had a standing arrangement with the quarrymen whereby he accepted fossils as payment for his services. When *Archaeopteryx* turned up Häberlein was not slow to appreciate its worth. He announced that he had the fossil and invited interested parties to view it and make a bid for it, but they were allowed only a brief glimpse of the specimen. Making notes or drawings was prohibited.

Häberlein's sales tactics probably drew as much attention as the specimen, but they had the desired effect. German museums wanted the fossil but were put off by the discordant remarks of the eminent Andreas Wagner. Meanwhile Richard Owen, by then curator of the

Archaeopteryx: from the moment of discovery in 1861, the fossil evidence of reptilian claws and teeth combined with bird-like feathers was seen as a unique example of evolution in progress. Indeed, because *Archaeopteryx* was so significant, some anti-evolutionists tried to show that it was a fake.

British Museum's natural history collections, sent a geologist, George Waterhouse, to Pappenheim to negotiate. Waterhouse bought *Archaeopteryx*, along with another 1,702 specimens from Häberlein's collections, for a total of £700. Häberlein is said to have used the money as a dowry for his daughter.

Fifteen years later another specimen of *Archaeopteryx* was found in a quarry at Eichstätt, a short distance from Solenhofen. By this time the old doctor had died but his son acquired the fossil and handled the financial negotiations. The asking price was 36,000 gold marks. After four years of haggling the specimen went to the Berlin Museum for 20,000 marks.

For some years both the British and the Berlin specimens were deemed to represent the same species, but in the 1920s a German paleontologist decided that the Berlin specimen was different enough to be assigned to a whole new genus, which he called *Archaeornis*. Furthermore, he said, *Archaeornis* alone was the ancestor of all the modern birds except the ostriches and their kind which, in his view, were descended from the British Museum's *Archaeopteryx*. This generic distinction prevailed in Germany during the twenties and thirties, but eventually faded before a growing consensus of opinion that the specimens were generically identical. Subsequently three more specimens were identified, the last only in 1973, when a fossil previously described as a pterosaur was found to have feathers too. Today all five specimens are ascribed to the same genus – *Archaeopteryx*.

The British Museum's *Archaeopteryx* arrived in London in October 1862 and the following month Richard Owen presented a formal description of the specimen in a paper read before the Royal Society. Owen was as cautious as one might expect of a man who struggled against the tide of evolutionary theory throughout his career. He declared the specimen 'unequivocally . . . a bird, with rare peculiarities indicative of a distinct order in that class'.

Others were less cautious: 'startling', 'marvellous', 'a sensation', 'wonderful discovery', commented various authors in the journals, generally conveying the view that *Archaeopteryx* was of 'extreme importance as bearing upon the great question of the origin of species', tending to 'link together the two great classes of Birds and Reptiles . . .'

This link was strengthened during December 1862 when John Evans, an expert on ancient stone implements, examined the slabs containing the *Archaeopteryx* fossil and claimed to discern fragments of a beak with four teeth, a distinctly reptilian feature which Owen had overlooked and now dismissed as the mouth of some fish, fossilized along with *Archaeopteryx*. But others inclined to agree with Evans, and Hugh Falconer, who was secretary of the Royal Society, greeted his correction of Owen's omission with glee. He wrote to Evans:

'Hail, Prince of Audacious Paleontologists! Tell me all about it. I hear that you have today discovered the *teeth* and jaws of the *Archaeopteryx*. To-morrow I expect to hear of your having found the liver and lights! And who knows, but that in the long run, you may get hold of the *fossil song* of the same creature, impressed by harmonic variation on the matrix. But keep your own counsel, and do not let yourself by blarneyed out of it.'

Archaeopteryx is probably the most famous fossil ever found, and certainly one of the most important in terms of evolutionary theory. There is no other fossil which quite so precisely defines an intermediate stage between one class of animal and another. Its pelvis is birdlike; its toes would have enabled the creature to perch on branches like modern birds; and the furcula (the fused collarbones) takes a form approaching that of the wishbone in modern birds. On the other hand, the creature lacked the keel on the breastbone to which the strong flight muscles of modern birds are attached; its bones were solid, with none of the air spaces that make bird bones so light; it had a long bony tail, claws on its forelimbs, and teeth. But over and above all these contradictory features, *Archaeopteryx* had feathers. The skeleton may seem a puzzling mixture of reptile and incipient bird-like features, but the feathers were indisputably identical to those of modern flying birds.

Given the significance of the feathers it is not surprising that they have evoked the occasional accusation that they were fake, impressed on the fossil of a pterosaur solely to provide evidence for the theory of evolution. The heat of scientific controversy in the 1860s and the financial dealing of the Häberleins would seem to provide ample motive for faking the evidence, but the sheer difficulty of reproducing convincing feather detail, down to fractions of a millimetre, on both inner surfaces of the split slab in which the fossil was found, soon ruled in favour of a genuine article. And the subsequent discovery of more specimens rendered the likelihood of them all being fakes even more improbable.

However, if *Archaeopteryx* provides convincing evidence of an important stage in the evolution of birds from reptiles, it gives very few clues to the process by which they came to fly. Feathers must have evolved from scales, but one of the first questions to be considered is whether they evolved specifically for flight or to help the creature maintain a comfortable body temperature, either by keeping heat in or keeping it out. The odds must be that the feathers were for flight; they are very complex structures and something much simpler would have sufficed to maintain body temperature.

The ancestral bird was probably a reptile-like creature about the size of a crow which took to climbing trees with the help of claws on its forelimbs. Even the slightest fringe of elongated scales or proto-feathers along the trailing edge of its limbs would have bestowed an immediate advantage when it came to jumping or gliding down again. Time – millions of years – and the evolutionary process of natural selection did the rest, and the birds have been flying ever since. Meanwhile the dinosaurs, who shared a close ancestor with the birds, became extinct.

Why did the dinosaurs become extinct? Despite a popular image of

Overleaf: the evidence of fossilized trails suggests that *Diplodocus*, one of the longest (typically 26 metres from head to tail tip) and most famous of all the dinosaurs, may have been a social animal that migrated in large herds between seasonal pastures.

lumbering obsolescence they were a highly successful form of life on Earth for a very long time. What went wrong? This is the question that paleontologists are most frequently asked and are probably least able to answer, although a whole host of answers have been put forward at various times, ranging from the sublime to the ridiculous: climatic changes, poison gas, volcanic dust, continental drift, floods, sunspots, gene pool drainage by little mammalian egg-eaters, suicide, God's will, little green men from flying saucers, lack of standing room in Noah's Ark, ennui . . . one imaginative suggestion even ascribes the dinosaurs' demise to the disappearance of ferns in the Mesozoic forests. Ferns contain purgative oils, it seems, so when the ferns went the dinosaurs lost their customary laxatives; apathy ensued, sex drive declined to bring eventual extinction from the inglorious effects of constipation.

Practically anything anyone cares to suggest as an explanation for the disappearance of the dinosaurs is quite likely to have been suggested already in the 100 years or so that people have been pondering the problem. Extraterrestrial agencies are often invoked. In 1976, for instance, scientists from the University of California at Berkeley proposed the impact of an asteroid some ten kilometres in diameter as the cause, basing their case on the discovery of the exceedingly rare mineral, iridium, at up to 30 times the normal concentration, in bands of sedimentary clay about 65 million years old found at a number of points around the globe.

Since all the Earth's iridium is derived from micrometeorites that constantly rain down from space, the exceptional concentrations identified by the Berkeley group would have required the very sudden arrival of some 500 billion tons of extraterrestrial material. A very large asteroid was the only feasible source, they concluded. The impact of such an object would have generated massive shock waves; it would have sent dense clouds of dust high into the atmosphere, enveloping the Earth and blocking out sunlight. Had it fallen in the ocean it would have created tidal waves eight kilometres high. The combined effects would have been quite enough to kill off the dinosaurs, and virtually everything else too.

And if an asteroid did not do the trick, how about the explosion of a supernova star, as outlined by Dale Russell in 1979? These colossal explosions in outer space initially radiate as much energy as ten billion suns, or as much as all the stars in the galaxy combined. If one occurred about 50 light years away, life on Earth would have been subjected to a sequence of extremely uncomfortable events. The initial burst of electromagnetic radiation would have arrived during the first few hours, followed between three and 30 years later by intense cosmic rays and high levels of radiation persisting for about ten years. Between 3,000 and 30,000 years later the Earth would have been enveloped by the expanding shell of the supernova remnants, and subjected to another 1,000 years of high radiation. Astrophysical calculations suggest that on average a supernova explosion might occur within 50 light years of Earth every 70 million years or so – but the dinosaurs were around for 140 million years.

Another point about cataclysmic explanations of the dinosaurs' extinction is their unacceptable element of overkill – everything else disappears along with the dinosaurs, which simply was not the case; many plant and animal species remained alive.

So, if these ideas are rejected, what remains? A plausible explanation stems from studies published in 1981, which showed that the Earth experienced a substantial and world-wide drop in sea levels around 65 million years ago. The effect was dramatic, not only on life in and around shallow waters, but also on the Earth's atmosphere and climate. At first the overall global temperature rose significantly with the carbon dioxide increase that followed the demise of many photosynthesizing plants (which normally absorb large quantities of the gas), but it began to fall again and continued to fall for a very long time, effecting a gradual and progressive changeover in both vegetation and fauna that proceeded from the poles towards the equator. Moist tropical forests were gradually replaced by woodland of a more temperate kind. The fossil record shows that the fate of the dinosaurs followed the retreat of tropical vegetation towards the equator. None adapted to the changeover. Species first disappeared in northerly latitudes, and the last of them much nearer the equator.

In considering this solution it is important to bear in mind that extinction is a vital fact of life on Earth, not an odd aberrant incident. Indeed, the evolutionary progression could not continue if some forms did not become extinct, there simply would not be room. The fossil record shows that for every species alive today there have been at least nine that became extinct. Some respected authorities say that probably more than 99.99999 per cent of all the species that have ever existed on Earth are now extinct, and many of these have disappeared no less abruptly than the dinosaurs (although their disappearance was hardly an overnight affair – it was more a numerical decline to zero and as such spanned several million years).

Also, because the dinosaurs were the largest land creatures to have inhabited the Earth, our view of their extinction has become distorted. Size impresses mortals, but in terms of life and extinction being the largest is really no different from being the fastest, slowest, fattest, skinniest or smallest creature ever to have become extinct.

To sum up, the dinosaurs were very specialized in their ways of life and, for reasons as yet not understood, they simply did not undergo the evolutionary developments that were needed for survival in their changing world. But the dinosaurs did not leave the Earth unpopulated; as their numbers declined, others increased.

Nat. size.

PHASCOLOTHERIUM BUCKLANDI.

Chapter Six

THE FIRST MAMMALS

advent of a special talent

In the 1790s the French anatomist Georges Cuvier (top left) defined the anatomical procedures that enabled him to reconstruct extinct animals such as *Megatherium* (top) from the evidence of fossil bones. The tiny jaw (seen through a magnifying glass) was brought to Cuvier's attention by William Buckland (foreground left), professor of geology at Oxford University. Found in deposits that had also contained the remains of a large dinosaur's toe-bone (foreground right), the jaw had definite mammalian affinities, indicating that mammals had existed in more ancient times than anyone had supposed.

There are about 4,500 species of mammals on Earth and they come in all shapes and sizes – from the tiny shrew to the elephant, from the mole to the whale, tigers, dogs, squirrels, giraffes, bears and, of course, people. The mammals are a diverse group, certainly the most conspicuously successful animals on Earth. They have crawled, climbed, run, burrowed and swum their way into all the major habitats that the Earth has to offer.

The mammals are very active, consciously aware of their surroundings, often inquisitive, and always protective of their young. All mammals suckle the new-born. They all share, to a greater or lesser extent, the inheritance of a brain that is capable of performing more than just the instinctive responses that their ancestors required. In primitive vertebrates the brain was little more than a bundle of nerve endings at the head of the spinal cord, which acted as a sort of central switchboard for turning on and off the power needed to activate certain muscles and bodily functions in response to particular stimuli. The behaviour of the animal was wholly instinctive, as indeed it had to be if the flick of the tail was to remove a fish from the danger its eye had perceived, or if the heart was to maintain a rate appropriate to the activity of the moment.

But in the mammals evolution took the function of the brain a stage further. The outer surfaces grew larger and denser, wrapping around the instinctive 'hardware' of the brainstem a layer of 'software' in which, to press the computing analogy just a little further, stimuli were processed, analysed and evaluated before instructions for action were passed on the muscles and organs of the body. This part of the brain is called the cerebral cortex; its evolution and progressive development endowed the mammals with the potential of allowing reason to override instinct and heralded the most complex structure on Earth – the human brain. It weighs only about 1,400 grams, but a single cubic centimetre of the human brain may contain six million cell bodies (called neurons), each of which is connected to as many as 80,000 other neurons. Complexity indeed, such as even the human brain itself can hardly comprehend; an extreme specialization, which arose from chance mutation and was naturally selected in the evolutionary process as a means of extending the existence of the human species.

All mammals have a capacity for reason that they employ to a greater or lesser extent. Given the significance of the brain in human existence, it is hardly surprising that reason seems to have lifted it above the purely functional role of keeping the organism alive long enough to produce and rear young. But that is all it is for, basically. And although the reasoning brain has done a great deal for people, it is not the only way of achieving the basic end, nor is it even the most ingenious or the most productive way. Wherever people go they take a lot of equally successful mites and other microscopic insects along with them, and flies and cockroaches are not slow to follow. The Earth today supports around 4.7 billion people it is true, but for every one of those people there are countless millions of countless different insects and other arthropods. It has been calculated that for every person alive today there are three-quarters of a tonne of termites alone, spread around the globe, munching their way through a full one-third of the Earth's plant production. We should never forget the insects. The human brain may seem to dominate the Earth but it would be useless without the insects to pollinate the plants that feed it. And, ironically, even the origin of the mammalian brain owes a great deal to the insects.

Quite literally, the mammals sharpened their teeth, focused their vision, tuned their hearing and found their agility in pursuit of insects, and from that activity there evolved the complex brain that is able to co-ordinate reason and instinct.

*   *   *

At the beginning of the nineteenth century, still a good while before anyone's brain was required to grapple seriously with the concept of time spanning millions of years, most authorities were convinced that no mammals had existed in Mesozoic times. Only fossil reptiles had ever been found in deposits that ancient, so deductive reasoning suggested that only reptiles had existed then.

In 1812, however, some new evidence came to light to confuse the issue. William Broderip, a geology student at Oxford, was visited by a stonemason who had found two distinctly mammal-like fossil lower jaws in the tile quarries at nearby Stonesfield.

In some ways it is surprising that these fossils were found at all. The two jaws are minute, about 35 millimetres long, with tiny teeth just over a millimetre broad. At a time when collectors seem to have been most interested in the large and the odd, it can only have been their exquisite beauty that attracted attention to these tiny fossils. Not much bigger than a thumbnail, delicate bone and perfect, sharp, glistening teeth set in fragments of warm brown tilestone, they are the kind of thing no child would miss but which you might expect a man to overlook in the search for bigger things. Perhaps the stonemason's daughter found them.

Not surprisingly, young William was reluctant to make too much of a fuss about the jaws. The Stonesfield quarry was a Mesozoic deposit, every interested party knew that, and anyone claiming to have found mammalian fossils there would be dubbed either fool or fraud.

William took the fossils to his professor, William Buckland, who recognized the mammalian affinities, bought one of the specimens and borrowed the other (which he subsequently lost), but was in no hurry to publicize the find. Buckland was the first professor of geology at Oxford, but he was also a minister of the Church who firmly believed that the Deluge, or rather a series of Deluges, had been responsible for all the fossil bones in the ground. He had been appointed to pass on the wisdom of the new science, not to confound it with contradictory claims. Both professor and pupil believed in the mammalian nature of the jaws, but because of their confusion they decided to hold back the announcement of the discovery until they had the sanction of the great paleontologist of the period, Georges Cuvier.

Broderip and Buckland waited a long time for that sanction, and when it came it was not without qualification. Cuvier eventually examined the fossils on a visit to Oxford in 1818 and agreed they were mammalian, resembling the jaw of the opossum, and published his somewhat equivocal judgement in 1825:

'... if this animal be really from the schist of Stonesfield, it is a most remarkable exception to an otherwise very general rule that the strata of that high antiquity do not contain the remains of mammals.'

Broderip published a paper on the fossils in 1828 – 16 years after he had acquired them – but few were willing to believe they were of such ancient mammalian origin as he claimed. At first the objectors argued that the deposit in which the fossils had been found was younger than Broderip claimed; and when that argument was convincingly refuted they turned to the jaws themselves, concluding that the fossils were so much like the mammals on the one hand, and like the reptiles on the other that no one could justifiably assign them to either class.

After that the debate came to a halt for the best part of ten years until the jaws came to the attention of Richard Owen, the anatomist of prodigious ability and energy.

Owen did not doubt that the fossils came from Mesozoic deposits. Looking at them through a magnifying glass, which cut off the surrounding world with its preconceived notions, he saw the functional perfection of the jaws. Here were incisors that caught and cracked beetles, molars that sheared worms into pieces. The single jaw bones bore the marks where strong muscles had been attached. Owen recognized the implications; the evidence was there before his eyes and he had the willingness to see it. As he told the Geological Society in 1838, he was in no doubt about the fossils' mammalian affinities – here was proof that mammals had existed in the Mesozoic.

Owen was then in his thirties, that decade when ability and energy are often most aggressively combined. He was already known in some circles as 'Britain's Cuvier', and since Cuvier had died in 1832 he was well placed to inherit the mantle of the great man himself. Indeed,

Owen actively promoted the idea (one should never imagine that personal ambition is absent from scientific endeavour). At the very least Owen was the beneficiary of Cuvier's pioneering work in the fields of comparative anatomy and paleontology. What might have been controversial to the established authorities of Cuvier's most productive years was to Owen established fact upon which he could build his own interpretative theories to explain the amazing variety and quantity of fossil fish, reptiles and mammals then being unearthed around the world. Owen's theories were bound by the rigorous scientific discipline he had inherited but they were also indelibly coloured by the beliefs of the society into which he had been born.

Owen is popularly presented as a dogmatic and devious man who did everything he could to obstruct the promulgation and acceptance of Darwin's theory of evolution. Some of this is true, but there is a deeper truth. Richard Owen's career spanned one of the most tumultuous divides that science and society have ever witnessed. When Owen started out science was led by men who believed God was the creator and arbiter of life on Earth. By the time Owen's career came to an end, his field was dominated by men who accepted the theory of evolution as fact and declared that life was directed by natural selection, not divine ordination.

Although discomforted by the direction science had taken, many of Owen's contemporaries managed to adapt with the changing times and came to accept the evolutionists' point of view, even though few ever wholeheartedly embraced it. But Owen never changed; he stuck doggedly to his own interpretations while reasoning men demolished them around him. And ironically, as the exalted 'British Cuvier', Owen had even contributed to the strength of the evolutionist position by providing the formal descriptions of a good deal of the fossil evidence upon which their conclusions were based. He defined the distinctive features of the South American fossils that Darwin had collected on the voyage of the *Beagle*, for instance, and when on the basis of Broderip's fossils he stated so unequivocally that small insectivorous mammals had lived alongside the most ancient dinosaurs, he considerably extended the period of time that science had previously left available for the evolution of the mammals.

*   *   *

The first reaction of any lay person encountering a therapsid (the mammal-like reptiles whose role in the story of life is outlined in chapter 5) would probably be to hasten to some safe and distant place. Large, rotund, stocky creatures, with short legs, powerful stubby tails and large heads, often with protruding fangs, the mammal-like reptiles were distinctly unattractive – imagine a cross between a hippopotamus and a crocodile – but they were undoubtedly the ancestors of all the mammals, including man.

Much of what is known about the mammal-like reptiles has come from fossil beds of the Triassic era (225 to 190 million years ago) laid down in South Africa when that part of the world was covered with an extensive network of large meandering waterways. The existence of the beds and the strange fossils they contained first came to light in the 1830s, in the course of military road construction work then being undertaken by the British government. The man in charge of these operations, Andrew Bain, sent case after case of fossils back to the Geological Society in London, where they were handed over to Richard Owen for study and description and ultimately found their way into the collections of the British Museum.

Owen recognized certain mammal-like features in the teeth and jaws of the predominantly reptile-like creatures from South Africa and for 30 years or more produced a steady stream of papers describing a transitional state that evolutionary theory could have explained, although Owen chose to interpret the transitional features somewhat differently. By the late nineteenth century large numbers of mammal-like reptiles of all shapes and sizes were known in some detail; dozens of species and genera had been named, but the classification was hopelessly confused and their evolutionary development through time had yet to be defined.

The man who brought order to this state of affairs was Dr Robert Broom, an impish Scotsman born in 1866, who liked to think of himself as the scientific son of Richard Owen. In June 1890, two years before he died, Owen wrote to Broom:

> 'I cannot help foreseeing that you will leave – life and health being spared – a lasting name in the promotion of our common science.'

Broom lived to the age of 84 and did leave his mark on the science of paleontology, but it is a noted fact that anyone remembering him will almost invariably speak first of another attribute – his copulatory proclivities. Broom loved ladies and there are enough first-hand accounts to suggest that he let pass few opportunities of getting to know them intimately. It is told how more than once Broom was chased by irate husbands from remote farmhouses, where he had been pursuing interests more immediately mammalian than the fossils he was visiting the farms to collect. During an interview in 1978 Professor Sidney Haughton, a pioneer of South African geology, flushed and shook with anger as he described a visit Dr Broom once paid on Mrs Haughton while he was out of town. Professor Haughton was 90 years old at the time of the interview and the event he spoke of had occurred nearly 50 years before.

Sharp intellect and boundless energy characterized all Broom's endeavours. A bachelor of medicine and master of surgery by the age of 23, he arrived in South Africa in 1897 after a seven-year stay in Australia. By 1900 he had already given up a successful practice in Port Elizabeth and had moved to the Karroo, where medicine was less demanding and fossils more accessible.

By the 1920s Broom had supplemented Richard Owen's work with

Overleaf: the size and shape of fossil bones, together with the marks showing where muscles were attached to them, permit accurate reconstruction of extinct animals. *Dimetrodon* was a mammal-like reptile that lived in Permian times (270 to 225 million years ago), when the early conifer *Walchia* appeared amid the tree ferns and horsetails. *Dimetrodon* was not warm-blooded, but its 'sail' probably served as a means of temperature regulation by radiating or absorbing heat as required.

enough specimens and publications to confirm and clarify the transitory status of the mammal-like reptiles. He was elected a Fellow of the Royal Society in 1920, and awarded the Society's Royal Medal in 1928 for his work on the origin of the mammals.

The differences between reptile and mammal that had to be bridged in the evolution of one from the other are considerable. Reptiles are cold-blooded and rely solely on external heat sources to raise their body temperature to the level required for activity; they have to warm up every morning before they can start the daily round, and rapidly lose heat at nightfall because they lack insulation (it would impede the uptake of heat in the morning). Mammals, on the other hand, generate heat internally (they are warm-blooded) and retain it with insulating fats and furs; a consistent body temperature means that mammals can sustain a higher and more continuous level of activity which in turn calls for greater and more regular supplies of food than reptiles require. More activity calls for a more efficient system of inhaling and transporting oxygen, along with nutrients, to the muscles where metabolism takes place, hence the larger lungs, the diaphragm and ribcage, four-chambered heart and circulatory system of the mammals. More efficient metabolism requires a more efficient means of removing metabolic waste material from the cells, hence the kidneys and the separation of the urinary and fecal excretory tracts (which are combined in the reptiles).

The mammals also have a system of reproduction which leaves the young to develop more fully inside the mother after conception and grants them a period of parental care after birth, when the mothers' mammary glands provide a reliable and nourishing diet of ready-processed food long after the reptiles have been left to hatch and fend for themselves. All this gives the mammals a higher infant survival rate than the reptiles can ever achieve and, equally important, allows time for the development of a more complex organism and the cerebral software that transcends the purely instinctive capabilities of the reptilian ancestors.

The features distinguishing the mammals from the reptiles did not evolve all at once, nor is it possible to put each of them in sequence in terms of evolution. They constitute a mosaic of features, each independently evolved and enhancing the whole, and all dependent upon and contributing to the most crucial distinction of all: mammals are quite simply more efficient at catching and processing their food than reptiles.

As Owen had observed, the teeth of mammals are adapted to cut up and crush food, and their digestive system is fast and efficient, which of course is linked to the high level of activity that mammals can sustain. Reptilian teeth, by contrast, are primarily designed for catching and holding their prey, which is then swallowed whole or in large chunks, to be digested very slowly. Hence reptiles customarily indulge in relatively short bursts of intense activity (when they are catching their food) between long periods of inactivity (while they are digesting it).

The mammal-like reptiles were already a good way up the evolutionary tree from which all the mammals stemmed. The cynodonts (dog-toothed mammals), for instance, which Owen first described and Broom later collected in quantity, already had the bony platform separating nasal and food passages in the head, which enabled them to eat and breathe at the same time – a distinct improvement on the reptilian condition that would show its real advantage at the evolutionary moment when mammalian young began to suckle. And between the most primitive and the most advanced of the cynodonts it is possible to trace the development of several crucial mammalian attributes.

First there is the separation of the reptiles' simple dentition into an arrangement of food-gathering incisors and canines at the front with a row of complex food-processing teeth behind – the molars. Opposing teeth of the upper and lower jaws formed cutting edges as they came together, and instead of simply piercing the food in a series of small cuts they sliced it in a single co-ordinated cut. Heavier use of the teeth at the back of the jaw shifted the emphasis of its mechanical actions. The capacity to open wide, trap and swallow was no longer so desirable; it was more important to have a sound point of articulation and strong muscles under the molar teeth. So the multiple bone structure of the reptile's jaw (it is made up of seven bones) fused into the single bone of the mammal's jaw. In the process the capacity to move both upper and lower jaws, and even to unhinge them to swallow large prey, was abandoned in favour of a strong fixed joint against which more leverage could be exerted. The jaw shortened, a sling of muscle grew along and around it; thus, for the first time in any animal, the vertebrate jaw was able to effect a degree of sideways chewing motion as well as the basic up-and-down action to which the reptiles were restricted.

These developments in the structure and operation of the jaw called forth some major changes in the manner of tooth replacement and growth. Reptiles, with undifferentiated dentition, replace each tooth at frequent intervals throughout their lives. Alternate teeth are shed and replaced in waves that proceed from front to back along the tooth row. Each replacement produces a slightly larger tooth, so that tooth size keeps pace with the growth of the animal. But such a pattern of replacement is obviously quite unsuitable for animals with closely matching upper and lower teeth. So a pattern of replacement evolved which kept the number of teeth and the overall structure of the tooth row more or less constant: each tooth was replaced just once during the animal's lifetime, and an extra tooth was added to the end of each row in the larger second set. This was the advent of the characteristically mammalian succession of deciduous and permanent teeth.

As the jaw evolved towards its single-bone structure, the now superfluous angular, articular and quadrate bones of the reptile jaw took on an entirely new function, becoming the tympanic, malleus and incus of the mammals' inner ear. The reptiles' hearing was based on a simple eardrum, which probably evolved from the gill cover of the ancestral fish during the shift from gill breathing to air breathing. Now, in the food processing shift from swallowing to chewing, the ancestral mammals acquired the resonating mechanisms of the inner ear, with improved hearing and sensitivity to higher sound frequencies in particular. Improved hearing called for greater capacity for processing the auditory information in the brain. The animals became more aware of their surroundings, more capable perhaps of assessing what was going on around them and of considering the implications of their actions. They moved just a little closer to reason.

Also during this period vital changes were taking place in the reproductive strategies. None of this is preserved in the fossil record, such things do not fossilize, but from the evidence of animals living today we know that at a critical point the mammalian line ceased laying eggs like reptiles and began bearing live young. At first the young were born at a very early stage in their development and immediately transferred to a pouch on the mother's belly where they found modified sweat glands secreting milk; these were the mammary glands that give the mammals their name. The young suckled in the pouch until they had grown to the point of being able to fend for themselves. These were the first marsupials, whose name derives from the marsupium, the 'little bag' where the young further their development.

Marsupials were first seen in Europe in the sixteenth century, when European explorers brought opossums back from Brazil. Around 200 years later when British settlers arrived in Australia they found that the continent was populated only by Aboriginal tribes and marsupials. The Aborigines had arrived by boat some thousands of years before, but the marsupials had been there much longer. Indeed, their presence in Australia (and South America) is in itself evidence of their position in the evolutionary progression.

During the time that the mammal-like reptiles dominated the Earth around 250 million years ago, the continents were still joined together as the gigantic landmass that Wegener had named Pangaea. Then Pangaea split into two supercontinents, Laurasia (Europe, Asia and North America) heading north, while Gondwanaland (South America, Africa, Antarctica and Australia) wandered southward. Later, between 100 and 50 million years ago, the two supercontinents themselves began to break up. In the south, Australia and South America were isolated, but they carried with them the mammalian fauna of the time – marsupials. In Australia evolution carried the marsupial line into every available environmental niche, where they are still found today. The marsupials flourished in South America too, but the opossum is the only surviving example. The others exist only as fossils, the remains of species driven to extinction when the Central American landbridge connected them with the evolutionary development that had been taking place in the northern supercontinent.

In the north, probably in response to environmental circumstances, the mammals had taken the marsupial reproductive strategy a stage further. Instead of transferring their delicate and tiny young to an external pouch they retained them in the body, in the uterus, where they received nutrients and oxygen from the maternal bloodstream via a remarkable innovation called the placenta. In this way the young could remain in the uterus for a very long time – far longer than a reptile's egg required to incubate and hatch – but much of the gestation period was taken up not so much with the growth of the infant's body as with the development of its brain.

During this very critical stage of their evolution the early mammals required more and more cerebral capacity for the co-ordination of their activities with the heightened awareness of their surroundings that improved senses of sight, smell, touch and hearing were bringing. The infant's delicate brain took a long time to grow and required the safest environment available, but the rest of its early physical development could come later, after it had been born.

It was in the placental mammals that the brain's potential to override or redirect the patterns of instinctive behaviour with which it was genetically endowed became a probability rather than just a possibility. The larger brain called for an extended period of parental care while the infant was growing. And the important thing about parental care is not only that the infant is protected from danger but also that it is spared the business of having to find its own food, as the ancestral animals had to do from birth. Finding food is the basic instinctive drive, and not having to exercise it directly (only to prompt parents) left the infants free to acquire and use other kinds of knowledge and experience. This brought the mammals the ability to learn, which in turn required more cerebral capacity, and still more time for the brain to grow and more parental care, with more time for learning . . . and so on, in a cycle of cause and effect which was to have profound effects upon the subsequent history of the mammals. One of the first results of this evolutionary development was the prompt extinction of most of the South American marsupials by placental carnivores, once the Central American landbridge afforded them access from the northern continent.

None of this happened overnight (over many millions of years is a more realistic timescale), and no other mammalian line took the development of the brain to anything like the lengths that humans have shown is possible. The others stopped at an earlier stage and used the brain to serve other equally effective physical specializations by which their various lifestyles are defined.

The emergence of all the differing physical structures, reproductive strategies and behavioural characteristics which marked the mammals' evolution from the reptilian line ran parallel to a progressive decrease in the size and number of their ancestral stock. The mighty mammal-like reptiles that had dominated the Earth for around 70 million years dwindled rapidly when the dinosaurs began to arrive on the scene some 200 million years ago, and around ten million years later they had almost entirely disappeared. All that remained of the mammal-like reptiles' evolutionary line by this time was the early mammals themselves. A very thin line indeed, but resilient enough to carry them through what is often termed the 'Dark Ages' of mammalian evolution: 140 million years in the shadow of the dinosaurs.

This period of mammalian evolution is dark not only in the sense that dinosaurs would have cast a large dense shadow over tiny mammals, but also in the opacity of the fossil record, which is distinguished for the most part by its absence. A scientist of the post-war generation has said that all the mammalian fossils known from the entire period would not fill a shoebox; an authority of the preceding generation consigned them to a silk top hat. This interesting example of changing social attitudes in science serves to underline a persistent fact of paleontology: fossil remains of the early mammals – unsuspected until the stonemason called on young William Broderip in 1812, and unaccepted for many years after that – are very rare indeed. Thousands of teeth and fragments of jaws, skulls and skeletal remains have been found, but more complete and informative specimens are lacking.

The scarcity of really useful, small mammalian fossils can be attributed to their scanty chances of preservation: tiny bones are likely to be devoured, broken or decayed long before they can be fossilized. But larger bones are more readily preserved, and their absence from among bones so much smaller can only mean that there were no larger mammals present at the time. A staggering thought: for close on 140 million years the mammals were never much larger than a mouse. This means that only a very long, very thin line of tiny warm-blooded creatures connects us with our most distant ancestors. There is an uncomfortable feeling that a single misplaced dinosaur's foot could have extinguished the line forever.

Why the mammals never grew any larger during this period has yet to be adequately explained. While the dinosaurs diversified in such spectacular style – armoured, crested, spiked, clawed; big head, small head; short neck, long neck; mostly large, some immense – the little mammals hardly changed at all. There was little variation in size and few changes in their dentition during the entire period that the dinosaurs held sway on Earth. Perhaps it really was the period of repression that it seems, with the rapid evolution of the dinosaurs leaving little room for anything else. Whatever the case, it is certain that in the long run the mammals derived more benefits than the dinosaurs did. The dinosaurs are extinct, but the mammals are still here.

The evolution of the dinosaurs, though spectacular, was actually of a rather limited nature. They developed long necks to reach otherwise inaccessible resources, claws to rip things open, spikes and armour-plating to keep their own insides safe from other claws; and, of course, they grew very large.

The mammals, meanwhile, were confined to the only parts of the big wide world that the dinosaurs could not reach: the nocturnal world, which lay in the dimension of time when the cold-blooded dinosaurs were inactive, and the interstices of the dinosaurs' daylight world – rocky crags, forest undergrowth and holes in the ground. Here they

The early mammals lived in the shadow of the dinosaurs for more than 100 million years. Here *Megazostrodon* (foreground) lurks in the undergrowth while *Tyrannosaurus rex* (right) stalks the agile, ostrich-like *Struthiomimus* (centre). *Tyrannosaurus rex* was the largest flesh-eating animal that ever walked the Earth; it was 12 metres long and 5 metres tall, and its saw-edged teeth were up to 15 cms long – around 5 cms longer than the typical mammals of the time.

acquired talents that not only outwitted the dinosaurs, but served to outlast them as well.

The world of the small nocturnal mammal is immensely more complex than the world of large diurnal creatures. In the first instance there is the matter of scale. The small animal's world is relatively so much larger. Climbing in and out of a dinosaur's footprint, for example, would have required the small mammals to scale heights far in excess of their own body size – something dinosaurs were rarely if ever required to do. The mammals must have been at it all the time – shinning over branches, under roots, between rocks. Such activity called for agility and a high degree of physical co-ordination, calling in turn for substantial and regular supplies of food, which again was affected by the matter of size. Because their metabolic rate is relatively higher, small mammals require proportionately more food than big ones do. A shrew must eat at least its own body weight each day, for instance, while an elephant can manage on between five and ten per cent. Added to this, the small early mammals were carnivores catching invertebrates, which were rather more active than the vegetation the large dinosaurs ate.

There was also the problem of being so agile and active in the dark, which called for a high degree of sensory perception. Eyes became relatively large, hearing more acute, vocal cords more distinctively tuned, the nose more sensitive, and whiskers brought a fine sense of touch and spatial presence. All these factors combined to give the small early mammals an awareness of their environment which demanded constant fine-tuning of the integration between cerebral and physical equipment. This in turn provided the opportunity for adaptations of a unique kind: reproductive strategies, maternal behaviour, parental care, communication between individuals, learning.

In short, while the dinosaurs followed an evolutionary course that was concerned primarily with their physical hardware, the evolution of the early mammals concentrated on the software: brain and behaviour. This was a long chapter of gradual refinement that is almost entirely missing from the fossil record; a few clues provide a sentence here and there. But when the dinosaurs finally disappeared from the scene about 65 million years ago the little mammals were exceptionally well equipped to take over.

It was insects, worms, beetles and spiders that kept the early mammals alive. Teeth, claws and wits sharpened in pursuit of invertebrates, the mammals eventually emerged from the long shadow of the dinosaurs as small, quick-witted and agile animals with a placental mode of reproduction and a predominantly flesh-eating disposition. Incipient carnivores, they were ready for anything.

There is a discomforting observation to be made here. People like to think that the world is ruled by a natural order that mankind would do well to obey. Society reveres the peaceful intention and abhors aggression. Unhappily for society's moral sense, the natural order of vertebrate evolution seems to work the other way round: it rewards aggression and condemns the peaceful to extinction.

From the advent of the jaw to the arrival of the placental mammals, each new chapter in the story of vertebrate evolution has opened with a splurge of blood. The carnivores have led the way into every important stage; they have been the authors of every major innovation. The lobe-finned fishes from which the amphibians evolved feasted on their smaller ray-finned cousins. The first reptiles fuelled their development on the bodies of ancestral amphibians; the first mammal-like reptiles ate lesser reptiles; the spectacular radiation of the dinosaurs was founded on a plentiful supply of mammal-like reptiles to eat, and the ancestral mammals were descended from a carnivorous branch of the dinosaurs' prey, not from herbivores.

At each stage, once the carnivores have established a new theme in vertebrate life, herbivores have soon evolved with innumerable variations on it, it is true, enabling them to exploit their physical and behavioural potential to the full extent that the environment would permit. But although herbivores have flourished with such conspicuous variety and success, peacefully enduring the predations of their carnivorous neighbours, none has ever been ancestral to a further group on a higher level of evolutionary development.

Throughout the story of vertebrate evolution the herbivores' peaceful existence has led only to eventual extinction and replacement by some progressive carnivorous stock. The villain always wins, it seems. The villain's drive was instinctive, of course, but if the natural order of vertebrate evolution so contradicts the moral and ethical aspirations of mankind, where does that put human nature, the most recent phenomenon of significance to arise in the evolutionary progression? Man dominates the Earth, and certainly did not achieve that status by predominantly peaceful means. Are the aggressive tendencies that the species so often displays (both against its own kind and towards other species) an indication of human nature's basically instinctive, basically carnivorous origins? And if so, can moral reason, as a more recent aspect of human nature, prove capable of overriding instinct in the future of human affairs?

And what if human nature is instinct of a basically herbivorous origin? After all, although mankind is omnivorous, meat is not the predominant fare in the typical human diet. So is the peace-loving morality of the species an herbivorous trait that will lead to extinction, while allowing or even fuelling the emergence of some carnivorous offshoot that will carry the vertebrates on to the next stage of their evolutionary development? There is plenty of room for speculation, and but little comfort in the observation that we as individuals will not be around to see the outcome.

CHARLES DARWIN.

Chapter Seven

════ FLORA AND FAUNA ════
burgeoning opportunities

Charles Darwin's contention that natural selection played a fundamental role in the origin of species derived much of its substance from his observations of birds and flowers, especially during the voyage of the *Beagle* (notebooks, bottom right). The magnolia is believed to resemble most closely the earliest of the flowering plants.

Not many structural changes were needed to adapt the ancestral placental mammal from an insectivorous to a wholly carnivorous way of life. The large stabbing canines and sharp cheek teeth that had dealt so well with the external skeletons of invertebrates would work equally well when it came to attacking and ripping the flesh from animals with internal skeletons, and the action would soon be refined with the evolution of the carnassials, the pairs of teeth on each side of the jaw with long sharp ridges that act like shears when upper and lower teeth are brought into contact.

The animals possessed a very good set of general attributes: agility, sinuous backs, firm strong legs, sharp claws and acute senses. They were poised to adapt in a number of directions, unlimited by the restraints that specialization imposes along with its benefits. As an example of the limitations of specialized equipment one might cite the flamingo, which has a bill specially adapted to strain algae from lake water. It does very well as long as there is lake water about with plenty of algae in it, but if the situation changes the flamingo is unable to turn to another food source.

In the case of the superbly adaptable ancestral mammals, however, it was inevitable that sooner or later some among them would begin eating others of their kind. They probably began on the marsupials; certainly the marsupials were soon pushed close to extinction wherever they were in contact with the new predacious placental mammals – and that, in the end, was virtually everywhere except for Australia. So it is reasonable to put the advent of the placental carnivores at some time soon after the breakup of Pangaea and the subsequent isolation of South America and Australia, around the end of the Mesozoic era, 65 million years ago. Thereafter things would never be quite the same again. The continents diverged, the climate became more erratic, the vegetation changed, the dinosaurs disappeared and the Age of Mammals got under way.

For many millions of years before the breakup of Pangaea the Earth had been in quiescent mood. No great ocean basins were formed, no high mountains were thrust from the sea floor. The land surfaces were generally rather flat and watery, their depressions filled with extensive swamps and lagoons. Shallow seas, in which countless generations of microscopic planktonic algae lived and died, covered large areas of Europe and North America. By the time the seas retreated the algae's tiny fossilized remains – called coccoliths – had compacted to blanket the land with a soft white limestone which was probably the substance that mankind first used to make a knowing mark on the world – chalk.

The chalk deposits are a telling example of just what time can do with a continuous supply of insignificantly small objects. A pile of 50 coccoliths would stand barely one millimetre high, yet their steady, unremitting accumulation on the ancient sea-beds has left south-east England, for example, with chalk deposits over 500 metres thick. Chalk is among the most distinctive of the Earth's geological features; predictably enough, the period in which it was laid down has been named the Cretaceous, from the latin *creta*, meaning chalk.

The Pangaean climate for most of the Cretaceous was mild, warm and moist with a notable absence of extremes, becoming warmer towards the end of the period. Land plants flourished; first the gymnosperms (naked seeds), and later the angiosperms (seeds borne in a vessel) evolved and proliferated, and they in their turn fuelled the spectacular rise of the mammals.

'That abominable mystery,' wrote Charles Darwin in reference to the evolutionary origin of the flowering plants. Their precise origin and early development remain a mystery, but their appearance and subsequent rise is well documented in the fossil record. At the beginning of the Cretaceous period 135 million years ago the gymnosperms dominated the scene. The first angiosperms appeared only some 25 million years later, but within ten million years they were set to take over, and by the end of the Cretaceous 65 million years ago most modern groups were present. Today the flowering plants constitute over 80 per cent of all green plants. They are the most successful plants that have ever lived, with more than 250,000 known living species, while all the other green plants total only about 50,000 species.

Flowers are the rarest of fossils, even rarer than the insect's wing. They are too delicate, too easily devoured or decomposed for their remains to be preserved with any frequency. In 1981, however, beautifully preserved fossil flowers about two millimetres long were found in Cretaceous deposits at Scania, in Sweden. The flowers had fallen in soft mud, which preserved their three-dimensional shape in the process of fossilization. Seedpod, stigma, anthers, styles and petals could all be identified. The tiny Scania specimens serve to prove the existence of complete functioning flowers during the early Cretaceous, but they are unique; the early history of the flowering plants is otherwise told only in the evidence of fossilized pollen, seeds, leaves and pieces of wood, with the evidence of living plants serving to fill in some of the gaps.

Petals evolved from leaves, providing first a ring of protection and then a point of attraction for the plants' reproductive equipment. The oldest-known fossil angiosperm leaf comes from Cretaceous deposits

130

in Labrador and exactly resembles the modern magnolia leaf in all the detail that is exquisitely preserved in the small slab of red slate. The most primitive of the modern flowering plants is, in fact, the magnolia, a woody shrub with flowers constructed of many separate parts and its simple symmetrical petals still not so unlike the leaves from which they evolved.

Basing their ideas more on supposition than on proof, most authorities now believe that a small woody plant like the magnolia was probably the first of the angiosperms. It might have arisen at the edge of the gymnosperms' range and, with its reproductive strategies established, would quickly have invaded their territory. Gymnosperms take years to set seed and produce a new generation; any plant which reproduced and matured more rapidly would inevitably take over and dominate available open ground before the gymosperms could get their roots down. These developments would have occurred in tropical climes, ultimately producing an environment much like the tropical rain forests of today, where by far the greatest proportion of the angiosperms' diversity is found. The rain forests support so many different angiosperm species because the plants grow best in that sort of climate and environment; they grow best there because it was probably under such conditions that they first evolved and gained supremacy over the gymnosperms. That was on Pangaea, in the mild, moist and equable climate of the early Cretaceous.

In preserving so much floral diversity the world's rain forests are in effect a museum of ancient plants, a point of reference at which one can define the early condition of the angiosperms and then move on to trace their evolutionary progression across the wider changing Earth.

With constant temperatures and relatively high levels of moisture the early plants would have been able to grow continuously, as tropical plants do today, and soon would have evolved the characteristic thick shiny leaves that restrain water loss and thereby prevent tropical plants from drying out and dying during warm dry periods.

But with passing time the climates became more variable, and as the pioneers extended their range on the one hand, and the drifting continents carried the forests themselves towards less equable climes on the other, the plants confronted another kind of stress. This was a seasonal alternation not so much between wet and dry as between hot and cold, and the main problem was cold. Continuous growth cannot be sustained without continuous relatively high temperatures, and a period of very low temperatures can kill plants just as effectively as a very dry period, and for much the same reason – if the soil is frozen, the plant is unable to take up water; it soon dries out and dies. So plants moving into regions where seasonal temperatures varied between hot and cold needed an adaptation that would see them through the coldest times of year. They found it in the practice of shedding leaves at the beginning of the cold season and suspending growth until temperatures rose again, when the protected buds would burst forth with fresh leaves and flowers. This was the advent of the deciduous plants.

The earliest flowering plants were predominantly of a woody structure; they were trees and small shrubs, capable of reproducing themselves year after year. But although they were long-lived, the spread of the ancestral woody plants was limited by the length of time they needed to reach maturity. A plant may sprout from seed fallen on new ground, but if conditions then deteriorate it will die before it can mature and produce any seed of its own. The ground gained is therefore lost. Clearly there was a niche in the early forests for plants with more opportunistic lifestyles; the kind of plant that matured more quickly, growing and setting seed in a season, sprouting when conditions were right, lying dormant when they were not.

This niche was filled soon enough with the evolution of the herbaceous plants which today provide the bulk of mankind's food and without which it is doubtful if the mammalian line could ever have achieved much significance.

The herbaceous flowering plants maintain no lasting parts above ground. They all sprout, flower, set seed, wither and die in a matter of months. A short reproductive cycle, that is the strategy which sees them through the vagaries of climate and which has taken them into every available niche on Earth. Some are annuals which mature and die in a season, ensuring species survival through the extremes of climate and season with a crop of seed. Others are perennials, which also produce seed annually but remain alive themselves as well, storing nutrients in enlarged roots underground after the parts above ground have died. The roots will sprout again and reproduce whenever conditions become favourable. Tubers, bulbs and seeds; leaves, flowers and fruit – the bounty of the angiosperms.

And it really was a bounty, a veritable basket of evolutionary adaptations expressly intended to attract and feed animals. The ancestral gymnosperms, having originated very largely in the absence of animals, evolved defensive, even aggressive adaptations, such as toxic juices and tough seed cases, to deter rather than attract the animals that later came to feed on them. In contrast, the angiosperms' strategy was to establish symbiotic relationships with the animals. Interdependence was the obvious alternative to the strategy of the gymnosperms from which the angiosperms arose.

Of course the flowering plants evolved some defences too. There was little point in attracting beetles to pollinate magnolias if they stayed on to eat the entire flower, seeds and all; and no point at all in allowing browsers to devour all of the plant's food factories – the leaves. So the flowering plants had their tough seed cases, their toxic juices, thorns and spines too, but overwhelmingly their evolutionary progression was one marked by cause and effect, bringing mutual benefit to both plants and animals – food for the animals and reproductive success for the plants – each group fuelling the evolutionary progress of the other. And with the disappearance of the dinosaurs, the symbiotic, simultaneous rise of the mammals and the flowering plants, especially the herbaceous flowering plants, laid the ground plan for the way the Earth looks today.

The carnivores were the first of the placental mammals to emerge from the shadow of the dinosaurs 65 million years ago; they heralded the beginning of the Cenozoic era – the era of recent life. By now, after the quiescence of the Cretaceous period, the huge forces contained at the Earth's core were active at the surface again. The continents were moving apart, heading at last for the positions they occupy today. The wide shallow seas retreated from the flat landscapes. As the Atlantic basin widened, the Andes and the Rocky Mountains rose where the American continents independently butted up against the Pacific plate. India broke free from Africa and drifted north towards Asia, inexorably elevating the floor of the ocean in between to the heights of the Himalaya range that now marks the boundary between the Indian and Asian plates. As Africa turned a little and pushed against Europe, both continental plates crumpled a little, creating the Alps and the Atlas Mountains.

These continental movements, combined with a more variable climate, brought the Earth a broader range of environmental potential than had ever existed before. The opportunistic flowering plants very soon evolved the adaptations needed to occupy nearly all of them; the insects were an integral part of this process, but the mammals were not far behind.

Carnivores were the pioneering innovators in the evolutionary story of the vertebrates, but the herbivores were always the pioneering explorers and colonizers. No carnivore can survive where there are no other animals for it to eat, so although they carried the vertebrate line into each new phase of its evolutionary development, it was the herbivores that took the vertebrates into new habitats and territory.

The first mammalian carnivores to evolve from the ancestral insectivores are known as the creodonts (from the Greek *kreos*, meaning flesh). They soon split into the two main groups that still exist today – the felids and the canids, the cats and the dogs – and evolved many variations on the basic themes of stealth and strength, but these were largely of a behavioural nature. With few exceptions the creodonts retained the generalized physical structure of their ancestors. The herbivores, on the other hand, required a number of special physical adaptations for their new lifestyle and for the habitats they were to colonize. On the whole they were irreversible specializations that would open up new territory, but at the same time would close the door on the herbivores' potential for major evolutionary innovation. This is why the carnivores, with their more general features, have always led the way in vertebrate evolution.

The herbivores' specializations began, obviously enough, with the means to gather and process plant food. The cheek teeth needed to be broader to grind up fibrous vegetation, and more durable to withstand a lifetime of such hard wear. Broad and high-crowned teeth with layers of denser enamel evolved. The digestive system adapted to the special demands of processing plant food, in which nutrients are less concentrated. And with claws largely superfluous – and even a hindrance to travelling any distance – the feet took on a form more

Overleaf: an early hoofed herbivore, *Phenacodus* from the Eocene (53 to 36 million years ago), runs through the stages of a transverse gallop. The ability to run evolved from the flat-footed gait of the early mammals; first the heels were raised from the ground, then the digits, so that finally animals such as *Phenacodus* ran on the tips of their toes, the toe-nails having become hoofs.

133

appropriate to the needs of animals moving about constantly to gather the relatively larger amounts of food that herbivores must ingest. The number of toes was reduced and they were held closer together, so that the animals in effect walked on tiptoe, each toe protected by a thick horny plate that evolved from the ancestral claw. The paw had become a hoof; and the hoof gives the name by which the mammalian herbivores are known – the ungulates, hoofed animals, from the Latin *ungula*, meaning hoof.

Just as there are two basic kinds of carnivore, so there are two kinds of ungulate as well. Those with an odd number of toes are perissodactyls, and those with an even number are artiodactyls, a classification that was established by Richard Owen in 1847. Horses and rhinoceroses are odd-toed ungulates; camels and cows are even-toed.

The ungulates were the most dynamic part of the great mammalian radiation that followed the demise of the dinosaurs and the rise of the flowering plants at the end of the Cretaceous. At the beginning of the succeeding Tertiary period, during the epoch known as the Paleocene (meaning 'old recent time') which lasted from 65 to 53 million years ago, the mammals burst upon the fossil record in great waves of territorial and environmental expansion.

As with every group of living things, gigantic forms arose wherever there was food and room enough for them. *Baluchitherium*, for instance, a distant relative of the rhinoceros with the long neck of a giraffe, stood nearly six metres high at the shoulder and was about nine metres long. Where space was more restricted, or food more scarce, smaller forms predominated. Everywhere, the animals' basic form and behaviour was a direct response to environmental circumstance, and where the drifting continents isolated sections of the ancestral stock there are a number of remarkable instances of the phenomenon known as parallel evolution. For example, the various types of cat, dog, rodent, pig, rhinoceros and so on all arose independently on each isolated continent because identical ecological niches favour identical forms. They did not migrate or spring from ancestors with genetic predispositions towards particular forms, as can be illustrated by the evolutionary progress of marsupials in Australia. Cut off from the rest of the world, they diversified to fill all the niches occupied by placental mammals elsewhere.

The same phenomenon of parallel evolution is found among plants. The American cacti, for instance, occupy the same types of environment as the euphorbias in Africa. The plants look similar; a layman would probably call the less well-known euphorbia a cactus, but the two plants are related only in their occupation of similar habitats.

Environment is thus the most important factor influencing the shape and size of animal and plant communities, and the nature of the environment varies in accordance with its position on the face of the Earth and the effects of the prevailing climate. When fluctuations in solar output or in the Earth's rotational tilt bring long-term climatic change, environments change too, together with the manner of living things that occupy them.

From the Paleocene into the Eocene ('the dawn of recent time'), which lasted from 53 to 36 million years ago, the prevailing climate over the terrestrial surfaces of the Earth warmed from mild to distinctly tropical. This favoured, indeed even stimulated, the rise and spread of the flowering plants and the fantastic radiation of the mammals.

Then temperatures began to fall again, and fell steadily if almost imperceptibly right through the Oligocene ('time of few recent forms', 36 to 26 million years ago) and into the Miocene ('middle recent time', 26 to 8 million years ago). During a period of over ten million years the average temperature dropped three degrees centigrade. The cause was the formation of an ice-cap at the South Pole, perhaps due to a shift in the axis of the Earth's rotation and almost certainly accentuated by the movement of Antarctica towards its present position.

Although a drop of three degrees in average temperature in over ten million years may not seem excessive, it was enough to bring profound climatic change to the Earth. But since the change came so slowly, there was time for evolutionary adaptation and change in the plant and animal communities too.

The first effect was to drive the tropical vegetation back yet again towards the equatorial regions of its origin. But now the flowering plants were the dominant form, far outnumbering the gymnosperms, and from among them one of the herbaceous annuals hitherto restricted to swamps, river margins and other open places among the trees, was presented with the opportunity of taking over entire landscapes that the forests left bare. The climate was temperate now, but this did not deter the opportunistic, small, fast-growing and fecund group of herbaceous annuals known as the grasses.

The most widespread and most familiar of the flowering plants, grass did not begin to make its mark on the landscape until less than 15 million years ago, 100 million years after the first appearance of the ancestral magnolias. The grass plant was a long way from the magnolia in its structure too, showing just how adaptable the flowering plants can be and introducing vast new environments of meadow and sweeping pasture.

The climatic and environmental changes that culminated with a flush of grass around the world in the Miocene have been described as a period of crisis for the mammals, but that is too drastic a term for changes that came so slowly. It was more a period of changing opportunities. Grass replaced forest in many regions and certainly cut down the number of habitats for browsing animals, but in the process grass actually provided more energy per unit area and could therefore support a larger animal population than any forest or dense woodland.

Trees and bushes invest a lot of energy and materials in the business of standing up to support their photosynthesizing leaves. They must build and maintain branches and tree trunks, so comparatively little energy is left for the leaves, fruit and seeds that animals feed on. The amount of food they make available is a small fraction of their total bulk.

The herbaceous plants in general were a marked improvement on the ratio of available food to plant bulk, but the annual grasses in particular were a great leap forward. Grasses use almost none of their bulk in support structures at the expense of energy production. Even their seed stalks are photosynthesizing surfaces; virtually the entire plant is available as food. The grasses grow quickly too (and continuously when cropped), they seed rapidly and abundantly, and their opportunistic – almost nimble – lifestyles rendered them able to exploit the small-scale climatic variations that other plants could only suffer under. Once established the grassland regime became, and remains, the Earth's most productive environment.

But exploiting the grasslands was not without its problems for the mammals. The meadows look soft and lush but in fact each blade of grass contains countless tiny crystals of silica, an extremely hard and abrasive material that would wear down the ordinary tooth as fast as a piece of sandpaper, and here the change from the reptilian pattern of continuous tooth replacement exacted its price on the mammals. With only their deciduous and permanent sets of teeth to see them through a lifetime, browsers that moved from leaves to grass for their sustenance as the forests retreated soon wore away their teeth and died of starvation at an unreasonably early age. Numerous browsing species dwindled to extinction during this period of change, together with the carnivores that had preyed on them.

Inevitably, however, the evolutionary process brought changes too; changes that produced animals specially adapted to the grassland produce – grazers. These animals had teeth with larger crowns and thicker tooth enamel; across the crowns the enfolded enamel stood up as a series of sharp ridges which wore down more slowly than the softer dentine that was exposed in between, thus maintaining a durable grinding surface.

With the improved ability to ingest grass came a very real need for improvements in the digestion of it. Grass contains a high proportion of cellulose, which is not easily broken down to release its nutrients. Rabbits and hares get around the problem by passing the grass through their digestive systems twice. First of all it is broken down by bacteria in the large intestine, then it is excreted and ingested again for the extraction of nutrients by the stomach and small intestine.

Other grazers evolved a more self-contained method of dealing with the indigestible cellulose; they developed an extra stomach, the rumen, and a unique method of digestion to go with it. After grazing, the ruminants, as they are known, rest in some safe place while the grasses are broken down to some degree by bacteria in the rumen. Then the partly digested material (known as the cud) is returned to the mouth and chewed again before it is sent down to the true stomach where the digestion process is completed.

Chewing the cud and its associated physical innovations arose among the even-toed ungulates and quickly established the ruminants as the most successful herbivores on Earth. They diverged rapidly into the groups that have given rise to the camels, giraffes, deer, antelopes, sheep and goats and their success eloquently demonstrates both the

The large, stabbing canines of *Smilodon*, the sabre-toothed cat common in North America around 30 million years ago, were a specialized adaptation that evolved to penetrate the thick skin of its predominantly large, short-necked and heavily muscled prey. The sharp teeth ripped deep wounds, and a slow death from loss of blood ensued. With the decline of large thick-skinned prey animals five to two million years ago, the sabre-toothed cats died out, to be replaced by ancestors of the modern cats.

efficacy of rumination and the carrying capacity of the grasslands. There are 194 species of even-toed ungulates alive today, but only 16 species of the odd-toed form, and of those 16 odd-toed ungulates only one is exclusively a grazer: the horse.

*   *   *

Studd Hill, on the coast of Kent, features one or two places where rocks may be found containing the fossilized remains of plants from the Eocene. On a visit there in 1839 a naturalist by the name of William Richardson searched the deposits with what he described as the firm expectation of finding 'some form of animal life, whether of beast or bird, [which had been] sustained by so rich a provision'. This was a bold hope – for the chances of animals being fossilized along with their food source are very slim indeed – but it was not misplaced. In the course of his visit Richardson found a fragment of an ancient animal skull, with a number of teeth still in place. Richardson had more reason to be pleased with his find than he could have guessed, for the skull fragment was actually the first evidence ever found of the earliest horse, *Eohippus* – Dawn Horse – although no one knew it at the time.

When the specimen found its way to Richard Owen (and most such things found their way to Owen by that time, as the ambitious and able anatomist consolidated his position as 'Britain's Cuvier'), he described the little skull, with relatively large eye sockets and small teeth of a rather unspecialized nature, as resembling that of a hare or some other timid rodent. He called it *Hyracotherium* – the hyrax-like beast – and its true affinities were not demonstrated until 1932, when comparative studies showed that it was identical to fossils of *Eohippus* first found in America in 1876.

During the early nineteenth century, while the horse still powered so much of human endeavour and almost certainly carried William Richardson to and from his discovery at Studd Hill, the question of the origin of the horse and its fortuitous, not to say perfect adaptation to the needs of mankind was to become an important element of the larger questions then rising so ominously from the observations of science: why were there so many different species of plants and animals, how had they originated, and why?

Until then such questions had hardly occurred to anyone. Every right-thinking man knew that nature was an orderly and wonderfully harmonious system, operating in accordance with divine laws which, though they might not always be easily understood, were never without purpose. All living things were purposefully adapted to the places where they were destined to live and were endowed from the moment of creation with all the physical adaptations they needed to function there, whatever the prevailing conditions. Perfect adaptation was the term used to explain the bewildering diversity of living things. Each organism was perfectly adapted to its ordained place and status on Earth, and each part of the organism was perfectly adapted to an ordained function in life. The eye, for instance, was so constructed because in that way it best fulfilled the need to see. And so on, with every part of every living thing, everywhere. The first natural historians filled volumes with examples of just how perfect the divine adaptations were, and explorers returned from foreign shores with ever more exotic confirmation of the fact.

For many naturalists active at the beginning of the nineteenth century perfect adaptation was no longer merely a fact to be observed, but also a factor to be sought out and employed as the explanation of observed facts. Cuvier called it the final cause, the condition of existence.

Divinely ordained perfect adaptation sufficed as an explanation of the living world until the study of fossil bones and their comparison with living forms began to suggest that some species had been less perfect than others. After Cuvier established the fact of extinction in 1796, many chose to view it as proof of divine intervention: the great wave of the Deluge sweeping the unworthy from the face of the Earth, although it did still beg the question of why any perfectly adapted creature should be deemed unworthy of continued existence. Cuvier himself found an antidote to these ticklish questions in the suggestion that the Earth had experienced a series of divinely ordained catastrophic upheavals, during which its physical features had been sculpted and its inhabitants annihilated, to be created afresh each time, equipped with all the new adaptations needed for a new world. Each upheaval had heralded an improved stage in the progressive development of life on Earth, his theory proposed, marked by the increasing complexity of living things. The modern world was calm because it represented the completion of the divine plan, the final cause: the emergence of man.

But neither the Deluge nor Cuvier's catastrophes satisfied everyone. Others saw more than just a sequence of creation and extinction in the coming and going of species through the ascending fossil record. Perhaps species did not come and go at all, they suggested, but were transformed onc into the other by a process of gradual adaptation that spanned generations. This suggestion had the welcome merit of explaining away the evidence of extinction, which remained for many an uncomfortable contradiction of the divinely ordained perfect adaptation they had been taught to believe. It became known as the theory of the transmutation of species, much adhered to during the nineteenth century and most notably set down by the French naturalist Jean Baptiste Lamarck in 1809. Animals acquired useful adaptations in the course of a lifetime, Lamarck said, and then passed them on to the next generation. Thus the giraffe, for instance, had gradually acquired a long neck as each generation was adapted to feed from ever higher branches of the trees and, over time, species so changed their form as to render the original ancestors of modern species quite unrecognizable in the fossil record.

But if this was so, countered Cuvier in an 1821 publication, traces of the gradual modifications linking ancestral and modern forms must exist in the fossil record, even if the two ends of the chain were completely dissimilar. Where, he challenged, are the intermediate forms between *Palaeotherium* (an extinct Eocene mammal) and the existing hoofed quadrupeds? This early example of the call for missing links that has so characterized studies of the fossil record was answered in 1851 by Richard Owen, in a paper describing how the *Palaeotherium* species of the Eocene had gradually been transformed into *Equus*, the horse of modern times.

The single link that Owen first presented was a fossil mammal from the Miocene called *Hipparion*, whose teeth and hoofs were of a form almost exactly half-way between those of *Palaeotherium* at one end of the chain and *Equus* at the other (later he produced two more intermediate stages). While the teeth of *Palaeotherium* were capable of dealing with all vegetation in general, and those of *Equus* were specially adapted to the needs of a grazing animal, *Hipparion* had teeth less generalized than *Palaeotherium* but still not as specialized as *Equus*, Owen pointed out. And similarly with the hoofs: while *Palaeotherium* had three quite distinct toes and *Equus* had just one large hoof, *Hipparion* walked about on enlarged hoof-like central toes, from each side of which there dangled the now redundant first and third toes.

Richard Owen's three-stage demonstration of the manner by which the modern horse might be said to have developed successively from the ancestral *Palaeotherium* was subsequently filled out and even replaced by large numbers of similar fossils recovered in the United States from deposits dating from the Eocene to the Pleistocene. A magnificent sequence of fossils, showing seven stages in the gradual change of foot and tooth, was assembled by Othniel Charles Marsh (of dinosaur fame), and in 1876 Thomas Huxley used the sequence as the most demonstrative evidence of the theory of evolution.

For many years the evidence of the fossil horses remained the classic example of evolution gradually building up the form of the living animal. The name for this concept of evolutionary development is orthogenesis, from the Greek words meaning 'straight' and 'origin'. The idea was that once an evolutionary development had started it would continue in the same direction. If there was a tendency for animals to become bigger, they would go on getting bigger and bigger. Similarly, trends in the development of teeth and feet would continue, regardless, until extinction intervened.

There is in the idea of orthogenesis a faint residual whiff of the preordained plan that Owen promulgated: evolution leading straight towards a predictable end. But, although Marsh's fossil evidence seemed to confirm orthogenesis so positively, it was eventually realized that the selection of such precise grades of development from the fossil collections ignored a good deal of evidence suggesting that the evolution of the horse was not such a straightforward affair after all. The start of it was *Eohippus*, a small rodent-like creature, and the end result was the modern horse, right enough, but there were several stops and starts in between and no one could have predicted the evolution of *Equus* from *Eohippus* on the basis of theory alone.

The horse has existed in a wide variety of forms since its first appearance in North America more than 50 million years ago. Extensive fossil evidence shows that each different form was adapted to a particular kind of environment and food source, ranging from forest and swamp to grassland. Several forms existed simultaneously, and although the selection shown in the following sequence suggests that the horse gradually evolved from a forest to a grassland form, it should be remembered that this is an idealized presentation.

The slender *Eohippus* (right) lived in the forests and swampland some 50 million years ago. About the size of a fox, its low-crowned cheek teeth show that it was a browser, adapted to feeding on shrubs and forest vegetation; four toes on the forefeet and three on the hind feet gave it secure footing on soft ground.

142

Marsh and others had scoured the collections for evidence that would support the straight-line theory, but the collections as a whole revealed a whole host of evolutionary adaptations, some occurring not successively but simultaneously, and all principally to do with the exploitation of the environment, not the attainment of some distant definable end. For example, the shift from browsing to grazing inspired the changes in dentition, it was realized, and the move from soft ground, where widespread toes were beneficial, to hard ground where hoofs were more useful provoked the changes in the structure of the foot.

It is now understood that instinct was the principal activity that spurred the horse along its evolutionary path. The instinct to find food in new places, the instinct to look after itself and its young, the instinct to flee from predators. Since then it has never needed much else in the

The slightly larger *Orohippus* (left) was almost a contemporary of *Eohippus*; although also a browser it may have been adapted to a less dense forest environment.

Low-crowned teeth suggest a forest or swamp environment for *Mesohippus* (centre), which lived around 35 million years ago.

144

However, its bulkier stature and three-toed feet imply a drier environment.

There is some evidence to suggest that *Miohippus* (right), which lived around 20 million years ago, was adapted to inhabit the boundary between the forest and the grasslands then beginning to develop.

way of mental equipment; even the most highly trained horse cannot be said to exercise a great deal of reason in whatever it does.

In his studies of the fossil remains of ancient fish, amphibian reptiles, birds and mammals, Owen probably saw more evidence than anyone of the intermediate forms that must have existed between one group and another, between one period of time and the next, and between one level of structural complexity and another. His awareness that recent and complex species were in some way derived from more ancient and simpler species was evident between the lines in many of his publications. Often he chose purposefully to deny it, but eventually he felt obliged to explain the phenomenon with a theory that would accommodate both the evidence of his science and the requirements of his religious beliefs. The successive development of the horse from the palaeotheres was fundamental to Owen's theory, which he published

Merychippus (left), which first appears in the Miocene around ten million years ago, had high-crowned cheek teeth perfectly adapted to the life of a grazer on the plains. It was about the size of a donkey, with a long face to accommodate the large teeth. There were still three toes on each foot, but the middle toe was dominant, and the others vestigial, indicating some adapation to running on hard ground.

   Pliohippus (centre), of the Pliocene epoch seven to two million years ago, was exclusively adapted to a grassland existence. A single stout toe on each foot improved running ability on the plains, while larger and more complex cheek teeth facilitated the consumption of abrasive grasses.

The modern horse, *Equus* (right), evolved in North America during the late Pleistocene and spread around the world via the landbridge which at that time

146

existed across the Bering Strait. *Equus* subsequently became extinct in America and was re-introduced by Spanish explorers at a later date.

in 1851 as *The Law of Progression from the General to the Particular*:

'... facts indicate that in the successive development of the mammalia, as we trace them from the earliest Tertiary period to the present time, there has been a gradual exchange of a more general for a more special type. The modifications which constitute the departure from the general type adapt the creature to special actions, and usually confer upon it special powers. The horse is the swifter by reason of the reduction of its toes to the condition of the single-hoofed foot. . . .'

The key point of Owen's theory was that the nature and physical structure of animals was preordained, not acquired in response to behaviour and environment as Lamarck's theory of the transmutation of species proposed.

Owen first presented his theory of successive development at a meeting of the British Association for the Advancement of Science in 1846, illustrating it with what he described as the archetype of the vertebrate skeleton. This was in effect the lowest common denominator of the vertebrate form, the stem from which all the various types of vertebrate animals diverged, and in fact Owen's archetype is remarkably similar to the simplest vertebrates subsequently found in Precambrian deposits: a backbone, ribs, and a mouth opening. In a series of drawings Owen showed how every bone in the skeletons of fish, reptiles, birds, mammals and man could have been adapted from the archetype. The successive development of the cranium, jaw and all four limbs is quite explicit; so too are the origins of eye, ear and nose.

In effect Owen's archetype theory provided a bold and authoritative explanation of just how species originated and were derived from one another through time. Based on the studies of fossils and comparative anatomy, it charted a perfectly believable course for the vertebrates' successive development, with the added benefit of discounting extinction – species did not die out, they were gradually transformed.

Owen set down this answer to the question of how species originated according to the dictates of his science; but in searching for the reason behind it he found no answer in science and turned to his beliefs. Species had an innate tendency to diverge from the ancestral form according to the dictates of a divine plan, he said, and the existence of the divine plan was proven in the very conception of the archetypal vertebrate:

'... the recognition of an ideal Exemplar for the Vertebrated animals proves that the knowledge of such a being as Man must have existed before Man appeared. For the Divine mind which planned the Archetype also foreknew all its modifications.'

And what about the horse? Owen had an explanation:

'Of all the quadrupedal servants of Man none have proved of more value to him, in peace or war, than the horse: none have co-operated with the advancing races more influentially in Man's destined mastery of the Earth and its lower denizens. In all the modifications of the old palaeotherian type to this end, the horse has acquired nobler proportions and higher faculties, more strength, more speed.... As such, I believe the Horse to have been predestined and prepared for Man.'

Even the space between the incisors and the molars in the jaw of the modern horse seemed to have been specially prepared to accommodate the bit, he added.

*   *   *

Back in the forests, there was a descendant of the tiny insectivorous creatures that had carried the mammalian line through the long shadow of the dinosaurs, and in these animals the burgeoning capacity of reason was to have immense significance. While other branches of the mammalian line had found their niches on the ground, these small furry creatures took to the trees and adopted an aboreal way of life.

The trees of the tropical forests offered a rich and varied diet – leaves, buds, fruit, insects, birds' eggs and nestlings – but they placed unusual demands upon their earliest mammalian occupants. The animals had to be agile and strong, but more important than the physical demands were the mental requirements. Life in the trees called for a shift in the emphasis of environmental awareness, and an unprecedented degree of sensory and physical co-ordination. Although the nose had probably been the most useful sensory organ of the early ground-dwelling mammals, sniffing out food and giving advance warning of approaching enemies, in the trees the eyes were much more important. Because a tree is a restricted and potentially dangerous environment, an arboreal animal must know if the enemy is in the same tree, or the fruit at the end of a safe branch. It must be able to see very clearly and judge distances very accurately as it moves about through the branches. Inadequate vision could be fatal, so among the arboreal mammals of the Paleocene natural selection must have quite quickly sorted out the species in which the eyes had tended to look forwards rather than sideways, integrating the two fields of vision to give a stereoscopic image of the surroundings, with perhaps even the first tints of colour.

Life in the branches also demanded a special kind of agility. There was much more need to move up and down, as well as around and about, and it was often necessary to hold on tight. The ability to flex the paws and grasp things evolved, and in some cases the tail grew to provide a fifth point of fixture. The front limbs became the principal means of holding on and were used to convey food to the mouth, while the rear limbs became more the means of propulsion and static support. Thus the animals became able to sit with the back erect, the head turning with a perceptive eye, the ears twitching. Sounds, differentiated between species and among individuals, became increasingly important.

All these things – vision, agility, communication – called for yet more cerebral development. A larger brain relative to body size evolved; a larger brain needed more room and some restructuring of the skull began. This in turn was affected by the kinds of food the animals were eating: fruit, leaves, insects and meat. An omnivorous diet requires neither the specialized canines and slicers of the carnivores, nor the grinding molars of the herbivores. A neat set of general all-purpose teeth would do. The jaws broadened and shortened, the face became longer, the eyes moved to the front and the expanding brain took up more and more of the room at the back of the skull: an interactive and interdependent suite of features evolving through millions of years and eventually producing the order of mammals known as primates.

Basically, the primates are distinguished from all other placental mammals by the fact that they have retained the four kinds of teeth found in the ancestral mammal (incisors, canines, premolars and molars); they can hold things between their fingers and thumbs; and they have two mammary glands on the chest, frontally directed eyes and a relatively large brain. They evolved from the ancestral mammals about 70 million years ago and are represented on Earth today by 193 living species, of which all except one are covered with hair.

*   *   *

Tropical forests are secretive places at the best of times, difficult to penetrate and concealing their inhabitants in a tangle of vegetation, but the tropical forests that nurtured the ancestral primates from their origins in the Paleocene over 60 million years ago are the most secretive of all. Unlike the swampy forests of the Carboniferous period, the dry conditions of the Palaeocene forests did not much favour the fossilization process and have left scanty record of their inhabitants. But there are a few fossil clues, found where animals died and fell in mud along a watercourse, beside a lake, or at a forest margin, and the evidence of living species fills in many gaps.

From its beginnings in the dense forests of tropical Africa, which then still lay at the core of the supercontinent, Gondwanaland, the primate line split about 45 million years ago into two groups – the prosimians (lower primates) and the anthropoids (higher primates). Time and natural migration spread these groups throughout the continental forests and some were isolated as the continents drifted apart. The lemurs of Madagascar, for instance, have been isolated for close on 60 million years; so too have the tarsiers which still inhabit the forested islands of Indonesia and the Philippines. On mainland Africa another of the lower primates found isolation of a different sort, in a nocturnal way of life, and their descendants, the bushbabies and the lorises, are still found there today.

When South America broke away from Gondwanaland the new continent carried with it into isolation a branch of the lower primates known in terms of their location as the New World monkeys and, more formally, in terms of their physiognomy as the platyrrhines – flat-nosed – in acknowledgement of their flat, wide faces.

The lower primates diverged and acquired distinctive adaptations within the needs and limits of their isolated environments, but they played no further part in the main story of primate evolution. Indeed, some authorities believe the living lower primates have survived only because isolation saved their ancestors from the competition with evolving higher primates which brought the extinction of their kind in every other instance.

The higher primates as a group are called the catarrhines – thin-nosed – acknowledging their thin, long faces, and soon after the isolation of the lower primates they split into two main groups, probably along the lines of diverging dietary requirements. One group adopted an herbivorous diet while the other retained more omnivorous habits. The first gave rise to the evolutionary line known as the Old World monkeys, whose living representatives include the baboons and the rhesus monkeys; the other group produced the hominoids, which are easily (if superficially) distinguished from all other primates by their lack of a tail and are represented today by the gibbons, the orang-utan, the gorilla, the chimpanzee – and man.

The evolution of man, as distinct from all other kinds of vertebrate animals, began with the establishment of the hominoid lineage between 20 and 30 million years ago. A shadowy beginning in the ancient African rain forests, but thereafter illuminated from time to time by evidence from the fossil record.

From the sands of the Fayum, just south east of Cairo, where 30 million years earlier dense tropical rain forests lined the banks of broad meandering rivers, fossil hunters over the years since 1961 have recovered the fossil remains of a creature known to science as *Aegyptopithecus zeuxis*, but more colloquially dubbed the 'dawn ape'. Jaws and teeth, substantial parts of the skeletons of a number of individuals, and one small delicate skull have been found – enough to reconstruct a picture of a small arboreal primate, about the size of a domestic cat, with a supple, sinuous back and long limbs, all four feet capable of both grasping branches and conveying food to the mouth. In all, the 'dawn apes' were a diverse and still very generalized lot in their physical form and could have been the ancestors of the hominoids. The brain was larger in proportion to bodyweight than that of any other mammal then alive, and there is a suggestion that they had already adopted some patterns of social behaviour that are characteristic of the hominoid line. The evidence for this suggestion lies in specimens of canine teeth that have been found. Female canines were relatively small and probably an integrated part of the working tooth row, it seems. Male canines, on the other hand, were appreciably larger and more suited to threatening and aggressive behaviour than to the mere consumption of food.

The next link in the hominoid chain was found three and a half thousand kilometres to the south, in early Miocene deposits on Rusinga Island, near the Kenyan shores of Lake Victoria.

Between 17 and 22 million years ago the tropical forests had retreated again and the landscape of what is now Kenya and Uganda was a mixture of forest, open woodland and grassland. The fossilized remains of creatures that had inhabited these mixed environments are often brought to light by the heavy seasonal rains that erode the gullies and ravines of Rusinga Island, and this is what drew two excavators, Louis Leakey and his wife Mary, to the area in 1948. At that time science accepted the theory that man had evolved from hominoid origins, but lacked the fossil evidence to prove it, and Miocene deposits were considered a good place to look for proof. On the afternoon of 2 October Louis Leakey was settling down to excavate some extinct form of crocodile. Mary never much cared for crocodiles, living or fossil (and the Lake Victoria basin is packed with both), so she wandered off to look for something more interesting.

And yes, she found it – the Miocene ape they named *Proconsul africanus*. First a tooth poking from the sediments on the eroded slope, then the jaws and some face bones. More than half the skull was excavated and carefully reassembled over the next few days. Some foot bones and an almost complete forelimb were found too. The discovery of *Proconsul* is one of several outstanding rewards that diligence and good fortune have brought Mary Leakey, but the discovery had an even more remarkable sequel. More than 20 years later paleontologist Martin Pickford was examining a long-ignored box of fossils labelled Rusinga 1947; it seemed to consist entirely of broken fossil tortoise shell, but among the bits Pickford recognized a few hominoid skull fragments. Amazingly, they turned out to be pieces missing from the *Proconsul* skull. It seemed that the 1947 expedition had collected from the same slope but had not seen the tell-tale tooth that caught Mary Leakey's eye in 1948. The Pickford revelation inspired a thorough search through all the Rusinga collections likely to contain more misplaced fragments of *Proconsul*, and many more were found – missing parts of the forelimbs, a shoulder-blade, some vertebrae and almost the complete hindlimbs. Now *Proconsul* is represented by much of its skeleton, a very rare find indeed, and other discoveries made since 1948 have shown that it was one of at least six hominoid species that inhabited the forests and woodlands of East Africa in Miocene times.

Proconsul in particular was a tree-dwelling, fruit-eating primate about the size of a baboon, unspecialized, with the backbone of a gibbon, the shoulder and elbow joints of a chimpanzee and the wrists of a monkey; quite unlike any of the living apes in its overall configuration, but a likely ancestor of them all – and of man too.

When the African continental plate butted up against Europe during the Miocene, about 17 million years ago, the event not only raised high mountains around the buckling edges of the plate, it also created a new landbridge between Africa and Eurasia. The climate was distinctly seasonal now; grasslands were spreading but woodland and forest were still a substantial part of the landscape. Most mammals were browsers; grazers were scarce.

The evolution of the higher primates, including man, was distinguished by the development of binocular vision, grasping hands and enlarged brains. Above the early primate *Notharctus* (grey fur, black face), are *Aegyptopithecus*, *Dryopithecus* and *Australopithecus*, whose eyes, in close-up, testify to his incipient humanity. At the top, overlooking two other inhabitants of the Ice Age, the mammoth and the woolly rhinoceros, is Neanderthal Man, his face lit by firelight.

The landbridge granted the African mammals access to Asia and Europe, and here the fossil record affords some more tantalizing glimpses of hominoid evolution. In Greece, fossil hunters found the remains of a fossil ape in deposits that were otherwise filled with the fossil impressions of ancient oak leaves and called it *Dryopithecus* – the oak ape. In the Siwalik Hills of northern India other expeditions found fossils of another slightly (and supposedly) more ape-like creature that they named *Ramapithecus*, and then another that they named *Sivapithecus*.

Dryopithecus, *Ramapithecus*, *Sivapithecus*, they all date from between 10 to 20 million years ago, and were in some way related to the evolutionary progression that led from the ancestral primate to man. But did they represent forms that had existed before the ape and the human lines diverged? Or had they lived after that split, and if so, to which branch were they ancestral – the apes or man?

From the moment of their discovery there was always someone who promoted the idea that these early apes variously or collectively represented the earliest known ancestors of man (every fossil hunter wanted to claim that he had found the earliest man), and *Ramapithecus* in particular was for many years almost universally accepted as such. But, as is so often the case with the fossil evidence of human evolution, the strength of these convictions had more to do with the evidence that was missing or uncertain than with the evidence actually present in the fossils. The Greek and Siwalik fossils consisted largely of teeth and jaw fragments. The jaws were robust, the teeth large and the enamel crowns thick – all features one might expect to find in a creature representing the earliest stages of human evolution, but hardly amounting to proof of that status. More fossils were required, of a more diagnostic nature, but when a partial skull and isolated limb bones were recovered from the Siwalik Hills of Pakistan during the early 1980s the evidence showed that the creatures were more aligned with the orang-utan than with the other apes or man. The consensus view now is that the ramapithecine and sivapithecine fossils probably represent ancestors of the orang-utan on its evolutionary and migratory journey that has led to the animals still living on isolated islands in South-east Asia, while the dryopithecines were probably close cousins headed only for extinction. The new evidence suggests that the evolutionary line had split before those particular hominoids reached Greece and the Siwaliks, perhaps around the time that the landbridge was formed between Africa and Eurasia.

The dismissal of *Ramapithecus* and his brethren from the candidacy of ancestor to all the apes and man leaves a gaping hole in the story of primate evolution. *Ramapithecus* might not have been especially far along the evolutionary path, but its remains did come from a variety of deposits between about 14 and seven million years old. Without *Ramapithecus* there is hardly anything between the *Proconsul* type of ape of about 20 million years ago and the arrival of a distinctly human-like creature that quite literally walked on to the scene about 3.6 million years ago. That is a gap of more than 16 million years. A long, long blank in which crucial developments and adaptations occurred, leaving few clues as to their precise timing.

The only near certainty is that these critical stages of human evolution occurred in Africa. Sometime after *Proconsul* the hominoid line split into the pongids, which subsequently became the gorilla and chimpanzee, and the hominids, which led to man. There were major climatic fluctuations during these times, ranging from hot and dry to wet and very cold. The tropical forests retreated to their equatorial origin, woodlands became dominant and grasslands advanced. And with the vegetation changes animal populations changed too. Many species died out, particularly browsers, and grazers became more numerous. From some small and perhaps insignificant niche among the trees the human ancestor emerged. The fossil record takes up the story again between three and four million years ago with a creature named *Australopithecus* – the southern ape – originally described by Raymond Dart in 1925.

With the arrival of *Australopithecus*, the fossil record of hominid evolution has a fairly well-established beginning. Australopithecine remains have been found in South Africa, Tanzania, Kenya and Ethiopia. There seem to have been a number of different species. They walked bipedally with the striding gait of modern humans, but stood only about 1.5 metres high on average; they lived in groups, it is believed, but used no stone tools and seem not to have known fire. Such slight, innocent figures in the dawn landscape of humanity. What put them there? Undoubtedly the australopithecines possessed all they needed to survive in their environment, but they seem so defenceless and their existence so precarious.

The human form is very special to us, but it has always been one of the least specialized among mammals. While other animals have evolved distinctive physical characteristics to further their species' survival, the hominids retained a basically unspecialized form. Humans can do many different things but they cannot do any of them especially well. No human can match the speed of a gazelle, or slice up raw meat with the ease of a hyena; they can neither climb as well as monkeys nor swim as well as dolphins. An eagle can see better, an elephant can smell more keenly and even a house-fly has a finer sense of taste. Virtually everything about the physical structure and abilities of humans would seem to have put the ancestral australopithecines at a severe disadvantage, so we can confidently conclude that their survival depended mainly upon their only specialized characteristic – the brain and its capacity for reason.

Chapter Eight

MONKEY PUZZLES

man's place in nature

Technology and culture were believed to have set man apart from the beasts, but science reunited them in the mid-19th century. Following the publication of Darwin's theory of evolution the British anatomist Thomas Huxley, and the German zoologist Ernst Haeckel, were especially active in promoting the concept of man's place in nature.

As the idea that species were somehow linked in a chain of progressive development percolated through the sciences and into the consciousness of society at large during the early decades of the nineteenth century, what stuck in most people's minds was the implication that man was a part of the progression. And – even worse – if this was true, then man's place in nature was right alongside the apes.

This was a nasty and unsettling thought to a society that believed man and nature were two quite separate things. The wild world of nature, 'red in tooth and claw', was bestial, animal – a state of living so undesirable that it served very well indeed as an example of how people should not behave, thus reinforcing the social and moral ethics of society. Even the goodness of 'mother nature' was a kind of bounty for mankind to enjoy. Mankind was the beneficiary, not the product of nature, people believed. And that belief, fundamental to society in the early 1800s, is an example of just how far the brain – the human animal's only specialization – had already carried man from his origins.

An integral part of this belief in mankind's separation from the natural world was that it vested power in a superior divine authority, which ordered the way things should be on Earth. This, of course, was another product of mankind's survival tool, the brain, and since it served the very important function of ensuring that people regarded themselves as all equally subject to laws that transcended the authority of mankind, it no doubt enhanced the chances of both individual and species survival.

But with the first whisperings of the theory of evolution the brain seemed to have come up with a dangerous and contradictory idea, taking power from the divine authority and handing it to the laws of nature. It was not divine law that ordered and judged life on Earth, evolution seemed to imply, it was the law of the jungle and the beast. Although every civilized person had been taught that the law of the jungle and the beast was exactly what mankind must strive to avoid, science was now trying to make mankind a part of it.

The implications were profound, not least for the scientists whose investigations had led to these awful suggestions. After all, scientists were among the most privileged recipients of the wealth and respect

157

that society distributed to those in whom it presumed some future benefit may lie, and wealth and respect could always be witheld from those whose work seemed to run against the mainstream of society's beliefs.

So, while there was a good deal of interest in the idea of evolution as it moved into the consciousness of society at large, the interest in itself evoked some apprehension in those conveying the message of evolution. In 1844, for instance, a book called *Vestiges of the Natural History of Creation* was published in London, assembling (and occasionally misinterpreting) all available evidence in a general theory that covered the evolution of everything from the solar system to man. *Vestiges* was very successful, selling nearly 24,000 copies in 11 editions in less than ten years, but it was published anonymously to protect the business interests of the author, Robert Chambers, and his identity was not revealed until after his death in 1871.

And Charles Darwin, who opened his first notebook on the subject of the transmutation of species in 1837 and had formulated the principles of his theory by the end of 1838, did not publish his conclusions until 21 years later, and then only when spurred to action by the news that another scientist, Alfred Russel Wallace, had recently arrived at the same conclusion concerning the role of natural selection in the evolution of species.

Darwin pondered his theory of evolution from behind the security of a private income; Chambers profited from behind a mask of anonymity; others, such as scholars and teachers, remained cautious or non-committal, perhaps spared the need of setting their views in conflict with either society or religion by their distance from the core of the argument and its evidence.

The man closest to the evidence, and about whom the argument was destined to whirl like some devilish and destructive wind, was Richard Owen, anatomist and paleontologist, and there is no hint of apprehension in his stance; indeed, there is every suggestion that Owen determined to make the transmutation of species an issue upon which his reputation could ultimately be judged – win or lose. Owen lost.

By the 1850s Owen was without doubt the foremost paleontologist and comparative anatomist in Britain, and probably in the world. His own work on fossils had provided compelling evidence of links and progressive development in extinct forms of life. He did not deny that progressive change had taken place, taking organisms from general to more specialized forms through the long history of life on Earth; in fact, his archetype of the vertebrate skeleton was designed to show how the various stages of the vertebrates were derived from one another through time. And on its publication in 1849 Owen's archetype concept found support in many quarters. Darwin, for instance, noted in the back of his personal copy: 'I look on Owen's Archetypes as more than ideal, as a real representation as far as the most consummate skill and loftiest generalization can represent the parent form of the Vertebrata.' A compliment implying that Darwin regarded Owen's archetype as a good representation of the real ancestor.

158

But that was as far as Owen could go. Although he had broken so much new ground and had led science to the point where evolution was a demonstrable fact, he stumbled before the intellectual leap that was required of anyone attempting to put the evidence of evolution in a theoretical context.

The evidence lay in the natural world, living and extinct, but Owen could never substitute a natural force for his belief in divine ordination as the power behind life on Earth. Man was a part of nature, he believed – that much was clear from the comparative anatomy of human and other vertebrates – but he could not contemplate the unavoidable implications of that relationship, namely that man shared a common ancestor with the apes. And it was on this point that Owen chose to make his stand, fervently denying any association with the apes and claiming man's quite separate origin and status on the basis of the species' sole highly specialized feature: the brain.

There is some irony in the fact that while Owen's work on the fossils was linking fish, reptiles and mammals in a chain of progressive development, his equally meticulous work on the primates was intended to destroy any suggestion of a link between the apes and man. Largely by virtue of having routinely received ape corpses from London Zoo for dissection, Richard Owen had become an acknowledged world authority on ape anatomy at an early stage in his career. After the gorilla was first sighted by the Episcopalian missionary Thomas Savage in 1847, skulls of the creature were sent to Owen for description, and he named it *Troglodytes gorilla* in 1848. Later he received skeletons and a carcass preserved in spirit.

Gorilla, chimpanzee, orang-utan, gibbon and man – Owen knew every bone, every muscle, sinew and organ of them all. There were more than enough anatomical similarities to suggest that all had shared a common ancestor, from which evolution, or progressive development, had adapted the general form to the specialized shape of each species. But Owen found more significance in the differences he saw than in the similarities, particularly when it came to the brain. The human brain was more developed, he said, it was 'an ascensive step' above the apes; the cerebral lobes were larger, more convoluted and possessed three features found in no other brain, he claimed, including the hippocampus minor, a small lobe to the rear of each cerebral hemisphere. Owen considered the allegedly unique characteristics of the human brain that he had described to be the seat of mankind's unique powers and status, and significant enough to merit the provision of an entirely new subclass of the Mammalia to accommodate the phenomenon of man as distinct from every other animal. He called this new subclass Archencephala, the 'overruling brain' and, revising the classification of the Mammalia throughout, went on to list all mammals in terms of their descending mental abilities. The brain put man on top. Owen wrote:

'Hereby, though naked, Man can clothe himself, and rival all natural vestments in warmth and beauty; though defenceless,

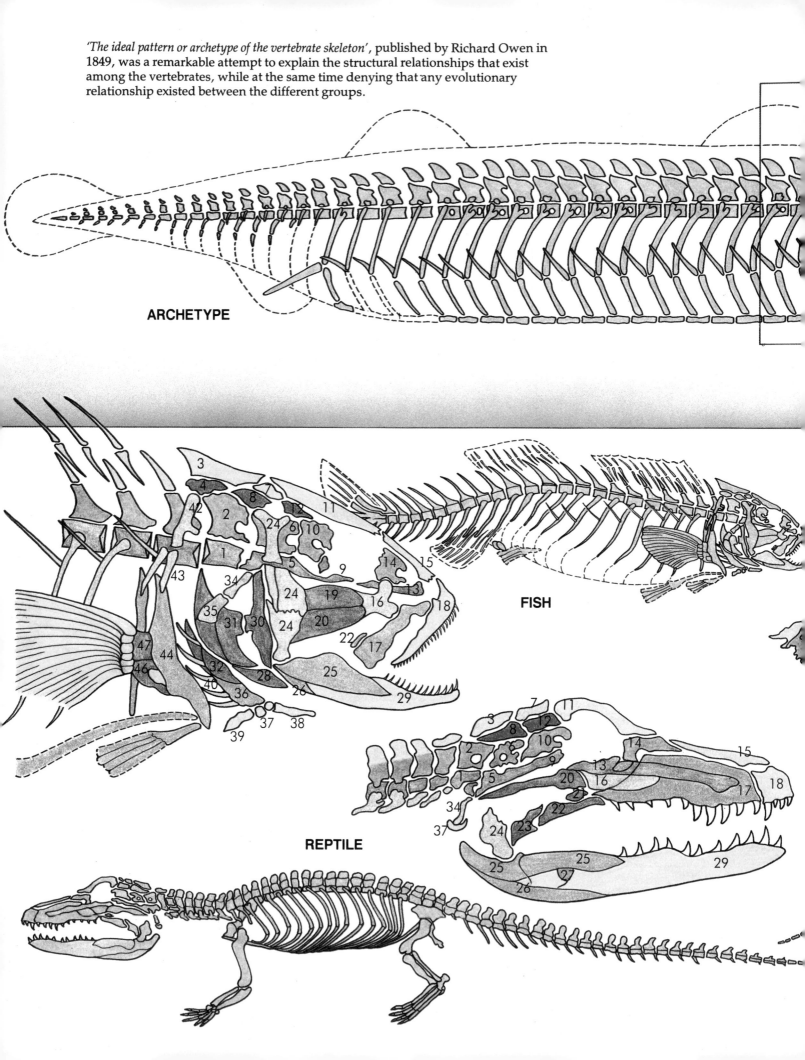

'The ideal pattern or archetype of the vertebrate skeleton', published by Richard Owen in 1849, was a remarkable attempt to explain the structural relationships that exist among the vertebrates, while at the same time denying that any evolutionary relationship existed between the different groups.

ARCHETYPE

FISH

REPTILE

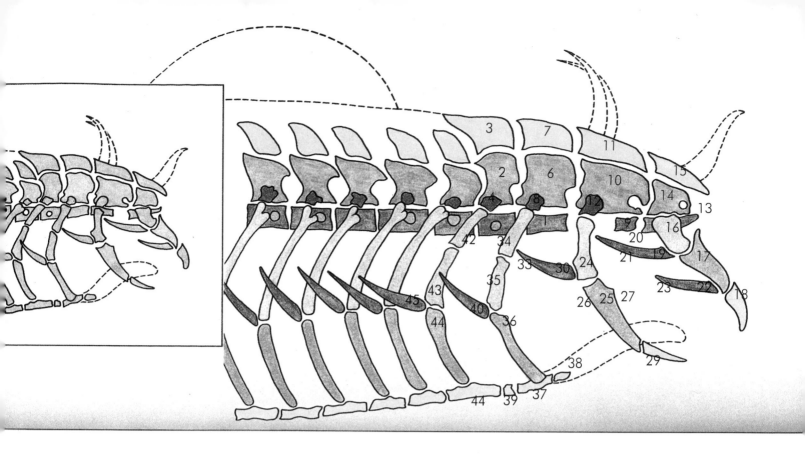

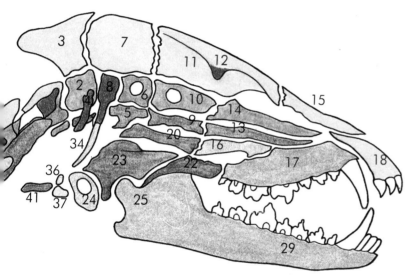

Owen's archetype was not intended to represent the ancestral form of the vertebrates. It was an *exemplar*, he said, representing the plan upon which 'the Divine mind' had based the modifications that characterize the different classes of vertebrate. The original drawing upon which this illustration is based relates by number each bone of the fishes, reptiles, birds (not shown here), mammals and man to the archetypal form, grouping them by colour in terms of their physiological relationship.

MAMMAL

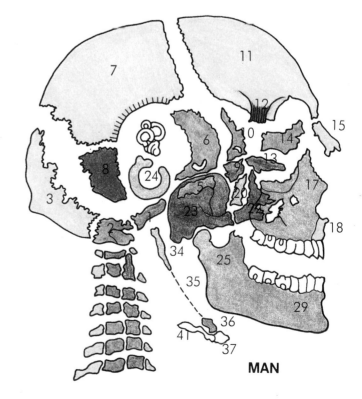

MAN

Man can arm himself with every variety of weapon, and become the most terribly destructive of animals. Thus he fulfils his destiny as the master of this earth, and of the lower Creation.'

Such extravagant prose might have been accepted and politely put to one side as a whimsical but honest attempt to reconcile scientific observation with religious conviction if Owen had not got his facts wrong. In the event, publication of his proposals in 1857 led to farce and scientific disgrace.

The trouble was that the three features Owen had claimed were unique to the human brain were all present in the ape as well, as indeed had been shown in the publications of other anatomists – Cuvier included – and ought to have been known to Owen. Exactly why Owen chose to build his case on such dubious foundations is hard to imagine. Some have blamed spirit-hardened and distorted ape brain specimens, or poorly supervised dissectors and draughtsmen; the less charitable accused Owen of attempting to suppress facts to suit his theory. Whatever the initial reason, Owen proceeded to compound his mistake by bluntly denying it. Thomas Huxley pointed out the errors coolly at first, and then with increasing vehemence. Huxley, 21 years younger than Owen, was set to become the genius of science in the second half of the nineteenth century that Owen had been in the first half. His erudite and eloquent attacks on Owen drew out the antagonism that had long lain simmering between the two. Huxley called on other authorities to support his contentions, which they did to a man. Owen responded with blithe repetitions of his original views and nasty personal attacks on Huxley.

The affair went on for years, eventually reaching the pages of popular journals as an hilarious argument between two very serious gentlemen over the existence or otherwise of the hippocampus minor in the ape brain ... one can imagine the tone. But in science it was deadly serious, a matter of black and white: '... one of us two is guilty of wilful and deliberate falsehood,' Huxley wrote to the secretary of the Royal Society in November 1862, leaving no doubt as to who was guilty and who was not in his view. Owen stood entirely alone; some tried to excuse him, but throughout the affair there was not a single anatomist anywhere that supported Owen's views.

Owen's row with Huxley coincided with the publication of Darwin's *Origin of Species* in 1859, the moment when evolutionary theory achieved sound scientific status. The row also marked the start of Owen's decline and the beginning of Huxley's ascent. Every scientist knew that Owen had played himself out of court and although he continued to publish and fulminate prodigiously, the game was now in the hands of younger men, for whom evolution was a fact, not a threat.

Owen retained the respect of society, however, and the power that went with it. He was appointed Superintendent of the British Museum's natural history collections in 1856, and oversaw the design and construction of the separate natural history museum at South Kensington. When it was opened in 1889 a large figure of Adam stood

162

prominently above the entrance of the museum. Some years after Owen's retirement a public appeal raised £4,500 for a marble statue of Charles Darwin to stand in the museum; since the cost was but £2,000, a similar statue of Thomas Huxley was commissioned too. Both still stand at the rear of the main hall, but Adam fell from above the entrance during an air raid in 1941 and has not been replaced.

*   *   *

Years before Darwin's book laid down the theory of evolution in definitive terms, all interested parties were aware that if man and the apes had shared a common ancestor then proof of the contention was most likely to be found in the fossil remains of an extinct intermediate form linking ape and man, which had some characteristics of both. An ape-man, or a man-ape. The missing link. Some fossil (and some non-fossil) remains were unearthed and put forward during the first decades of the nineteenth century, but no really serious candidate for missing link status arrived on the scene until 1857. Its discovery and description aroused heated discussion which increased with the publication of *The Origin of Species* two years later and rubbed yet more salt into the wounds then opening in Owen's reputation.

In his attempt to dismiss suggestions that man and the apes might have shared a common ancestor, Owen had stressed the significance of the brain, but he had also called upon other anatomical evidence. There were physical features found in many living animals that could not have been produced by the alleged evolutionary process, he said. The gorilla's prominent eyebrow ridges, for example, had no muscles pulling on them, and could not have been lost or gained by any aspect of the gorilla's behaviour, Owen claimed. Therefore the ridges must have occurred in the gorilla's ancestors and should be found in all that ancestor's descendants, including man, if the evolutionists were right. But ridges rarely – and then only feebly – occur in man, and this simple fact was further proof that man and the apes had not evolved from a common ancestor, Owen concluded.

How ironic, in view of such bold assertions, that the first fossils to qualify for consideration as a link hitherto missing from the line of human evolution should possess as their most distinctive feature the very thing that Owen had used to deny the common ancestry of man and ape: prominent eyebrow ridges. The remains in question had been found by quarrymen in a cave high on the precipitous cliffs that lined the Neander Valley near Düsseldorf. It is likely that the entire skeleton was originally dug out, but only some limb bones and a skull cap were salvaged. The skull cap, with heavy ridges overhanging deep-set eye sockets, has since become symbolic, its name popularly synonymous with the concept of early man. Known as Neanderthal Man, its brooding image of a shuffling, inadequate creature for a long time coloured and distorted the interpretations of human evolution.

163

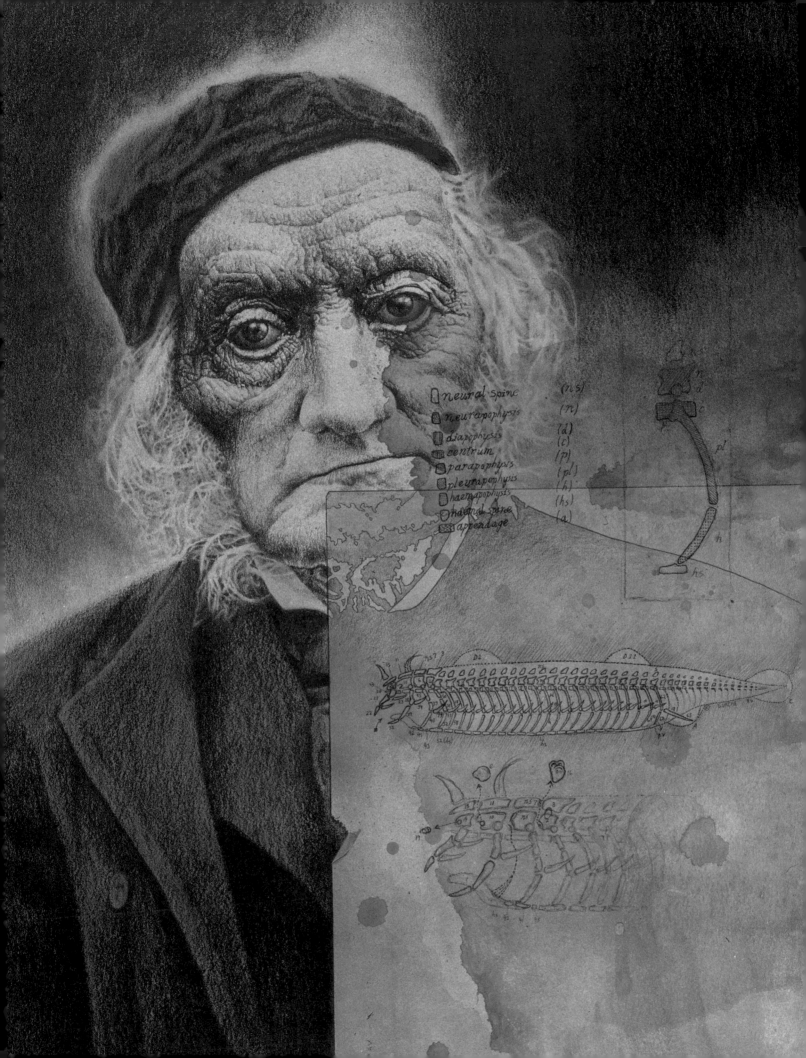

neural spine (n.s)
neurapophysis (n)
diapophysis (d)
centrum (c)
parapophysis (p)
pleurapophysis (pl)
haemapophysis (h)
haemal spine (hs)
appendage (a)

Richard Owen (1804–92) was the most influential paleontologist of his day. In his work he saw clearly that animal forms had changed through time, but while others saw the changes as evidence of evolution Owen struggled to explain them as a process of divinely ordained development. To the end of his life he refused to accept the theory of evolution.

Thomas Huxley included a description of the Neanderthal fossils in a volume of essays entitled *Man's Place in Nature* that he published in 1863. Since the volume also included a blow-by-blow account of the hippocampus affair it might have seemed a direct attack on Richard Owen, but its thrust ran deeper than that. Above all else the essays amount to the first definitive statement of the evolutionist position on the prickly question of man's ancestry. Darwin had cautiously tiptoed around the issue in *The Origin of Species*, noting only that by the study of evolution 'light would be thrown on the origin of man and his history'.

But Huxley, then still in his thirties, displayed no such reticence. Man's place in nature, the title essay made clear, was as a family of primates at the head of a series of gradations that led all the way from the lemurs, via the monkeys and the apes to man.

'I have endeavoured to show that no absolute structural line of demarcation, wider than that between the animals which immediately [precede] us in the scale, can be drawn between the animal world and ourselves,' he wrote. Anatomically, detail by detail, Huxley showed that the structural differences separating man and the apes were not as great as those separating the apes and the monkeys, and this being so, Darwin's theory of evolution left no rational ground for doubting that man had originated from the same primitive stock as the apes. His conclusion, however, was comforting:

'Our reverence for the nobility of manhood will not be lessened by the knowledge that Man is, in substance and in structure, one with the brutes; for he alone possesses the marvellous endowment of intelligible and rational speech, whereby, in the secular period of his existence, he has slowly accumulated and organized the experience which is almost wholly lost with the cessation of every individual life in other animals; so that now he stands raised upon it as on a mountain top, far above the level of his humble fellows, and transfigured from his grosser nature by reflecting, here and there, a ray from the infinite source of truth.'

And where did Neanderthal Man stand on the long road to mankind's supremacy? Huxley showed that although the fossils were the most ape-like yet known, they were essentially human and did not represent an intermediate stage between the ancestral ape and man. At most the skull showed some reversion from the modern human skull towards that of an ape-like ancestor. The determining factor, Huxley said, was the size of the brain. The cranial capacity of the Neanderthal skull was well within the modern range and twice that of the largest ape.

Huxley believed that the true missing link would come to light in time, but time has been less directly helpful than he might have supposed, for fossil man has proved very hard to find. Decades have passed between significant discoveries and even now the entire fossil hominid collection would barely cover a billiard table. Instead of supplying answers, the passage of time has mainly provided the space for hypothesis and argument. Not that there was much to argue about. With the theory of evolution gradually acquiring the status of fact among the scientists of the latter half of the nineteenth century, it was no longer a question of whether man had an ancestor in common with the apes but of how and when the species had diverged from the ancestral stock and acquired its distinctly human attributes. And basically these are but three: the enlargement of the brain; the habitual bipedal gait; and the dental changes that gave humans small front teeth and large back teeth while the apes have the reverse.

Quite early on the arguments shook down to two main schools of thought, one contending that enlargement of the brain came first and the other, no less adamant, that the feet had led the way, but for 30 years after the discovery of Neanderthal Man no new fossils were found that could throw light on the argument either way. Some fossils similar to the original Neanderthal remains were found in Belgium and Gibraltar, which suggested the widespread existence in Europe of a race appreciably different from modern man, but they gave no hint of his more distant origins. Meanwhile researchers, such as the Dutch anatomist Eugène Dubois, began to pursue theory in the hunt for missing links. Dubois took up a medical appointment in Java with the express purpose of looking for fossil remains of the human ancestor that a German zoologist, Ernst Haeckel, had said might be found there.

Haeckel's book, *The History of Creation*, published in Berlin in 1868 and translated into a dozen languages, was probably the first authoritative zoology text to wholeheartedly embrace the theory of evolution. In it Haeckel constructed the first of the now commonplace ancestral trees, depicting the evolution of life from the single cell through 22 stages of development to modern man, supreme at the top of the tree. Just down the stem, at stage 21, was the creature Haeckel proposed as the intermediate link between man and the apes, principally distinguished by the lack of what he considered mankind's most important attribute, the power of speech. He called it *Pithecanthropus alalus* – ape-man without speech. And where might this ancestor have lived? Haeckel suggested that South-east Asia was the most likely place in which the 'so-called Paradise, the cradle of the human race' might have been situated.

Apparently fired by Haeckel's hypothesis, Eugène Dubois moved to Java with his wife and daughter in the autumn of 1887. Late in 1891 the convict workers assigned to him found first a tooth and some weeks later a skull cap in excavations on a bend of the River Solo. Ten months later they found a fossil thighbone at the same site. Despite the circumstances of their discovery, Dubois decided that all three fossils had come from one individual. The tooth was chimpanzee-like, he said, the skull cap could have contained only a relatively small brain, while the thighbone was completely human and must have carried the creature upright. So here was the missing link, Dubois claimed. A small-brained ape-man that walked upright on two legs – Java Man. Dubois named his find *Pithecanthropus erectus* and spent the rest of his life defending his view on its intermediate status. A sad and salutary

On a modern museum bench a fossilized skull of Neanderthal Man (top) remains an evocative link with both the novelty of its discovery in Gibraltar in the 1840s (centre), and its presence in a firelit cave perhaps 50,000 years earlier (bottom).

story, for the fossils were too fragmentary and their association too uncertain to support such extravagant claims. But that in itself is a measure of the conviction with which one man supported the precedence of the bipedal gait in human evolution.

The conviction of those supporting the view that the enlargement of the brain was the prime mover in the evolution of man from the ancestral apes was most memorably demonstrated in a small collection of fossils retrieved from a gravel pit near the village of Piltdown in Sussex at various times between 1908 and 1915.

The Piltdown collection consisted of just four skull fragments, a piece of lower jaw with two molars still in place (the front end of the jaw was missing), and one upper canine tooth. But they were found along with fossil fragments of extinct animals and some equally ancient-looking stone tools in deposits that were said to have been of the early Pleistocene, or perhaps even the Pliocene epoch. This made Piltdown Man (as he soon became known) far older than both the Java and the Neanderthal specimens. Furthermore, the fossils were sufficiently complete to allow the reconstruction of the skull, which appeared to be that of a large-brained individual with an ape-like jaw – an archetypal missing link that seemed to dismiss forever the contention that bipedal gait had preceded enlargement of the brain in human evolution. In fact, Piltdown Man might almost have been designed with that purpose in mind. *Eoanthropus*, they called him – Dawn Man.

However, while many in England were inclined to celebrate the Piltdown discovery as further proof of their Edwardian conviction that Englishmen had led the way in human evolution as in so many things, there was dissension at home and abroad. The jaw was so distinctly ape-like and the skull so human in both shape and size that the combination seemed just too fortuitous, even for an archetypal missing link. Certainly, if jaw and skull had been found in separate sites no one would have dreamt of suggesting they belonged together. One anatomist claimed that the way the jaw and skull fitted together, as reconstructed, left no room for the gullet and windpipe; Piltdown Man would have been unable either to eat or breathe, he said. Another expert described the combination of jaw and skull as no less absurd than it would be to put a chimpanzee foot on a human leg.

But fossil apes were unknown in the Pleistocene deposits of Europe and as Grafton Elliot Smith, an authority on the brain and evolution, pointed out, why should 'Nature have played the amazing trick of depositing in the same bed of gravel the braincase (*without* the jaw) of an hitherto unknown type of early Pleistocene Man displaying unique simian traits, alongside the jaw (*without* the braincase) of an equally unknown Pleistocene Ape displaying human traits unknown in any Ape?'

There was really no answer to that. Despite all the obvious contradictions, the circumstantial evidence of his discovery left Piltdown Man reigning as the oldest man for much longer than he deserved.

More than 40 years later Piltdown Man was shown to be a fake. For some time it had been an anomaly, very difficult to reconcile with the evidence of subsequent discoveries and therefore consigned to what might be called a 'suspense account' – a problem waiting to be solved. Then in 1953 the patchwork of contradictions encouraged a young anatomist from Oxford, Joseph Weiner, to do as Sherlock Holmes had once advised: when all natural explanations have been eliminated, consider the unnatural explanations. Only that change in attitude was needed to solve the riddle. Within days Weiner had shown conclusively that Piltdown Man was an amalgam of modern ape jaw and modern human skull: a hoax. To this day the perpetrator remains unknown. Accusations have been made against most of the individuals involved with the original discovery and announcements, but none stands serious examination – the evidence simply is not conclusive.

The revelation that Piltdown Man was a fake caused quite a stir. The competence of the British Museum Trustees was questioned in the House of Commons, and raised a laugh when the Lord Privy Seal replied: 'The government had found so many skeletons to examine when they came into office that there had not yet been time to extend the researches into skulls.'

The Piltdown affair is an embarrassing chapter in the study of fossil man. It is most charitable to imagine that the whole thing was intended as a joke, which the perpetrator expected the experts to uncover without delay. After all, combining a modern ape jaw (not even fossilized) with a human skull (possibly from an Ancient Egyptian tomb) was an outrageous idea, even if it did so neatly summarize expectations at the time; surely he did not intend the hoax to go on as long as it did. But instead of tumbling to it, the experts fell for it and Piltdown Man was taken seriously for much longer than anyone aware of its true nature could possibly have imagined. This had profound effects on the science, not the least of which was the persistent belief that enlargement of the brain must have come first in the evolution of man from the ancestral stock.

Piltdown Man still held centre stage when Raymond Dart announced his discovery of *Australopithecus africanus* in 1925, and doubtless contributed to the resounding lack of enthusiasm that greeted Dart's announcement.

Dart, an Australian by birth, was Professor of Anatomy at the Witwatersrand University medical school in South Africa. Among his particular interests were the evolution of the brain and fossil man. Early in 1924 he found a most exceptional fossil among a crateful sent to him from a limestone quarry at Taung, in the Cape Province. It was an endocranial cast, a lump of fossilized material exactly preserving the interior form of a skull; not a fossil brain, but the closest thing to it. After death the creature's brain would soon have rotted away, but as the skull lay on its side on the floor of the cave from which the Taung limestone is derived, it filled to just over half its depth with the sediments accumulating on the cave floor. Eventually the cave filled and fossilized, and much later it became a quarry. Finally, this endocranial cast came into the hands of one of the very few people in the world who were capable of recognizing its true significance; another of the coincidences that highlight the study of fossil man.

A small, shining, brown object, the cast fits comfortably in the palm of the hand. Glistening white crystals cover the flat surface that had been uppermost in the cave; the lower surface, rounded to the shape of the skull interior, preserves in detail the outer form of the brain – blood vessels, convolutions and fissures – that had once filled it.

The cast was large for an ape, but much smaller than anyone had previously thought possible for the ancestor of man. Dart, however, immediately recognized features that were more human than ape-like. He delved into the crate again and found a piece of rock with the back of the forehead and face exposed, into which the braincast fitted perfectly. Seventy-three days later he scraped away the last of the rock in which the face was embedded and could sit back to ponder his discovery. There were no great eyebrow ridges, nor did the jaw jut forward. The large brain had not belonged to a large adult ape, it turned out, but to an infant with rounded forehead, a full set of deciduous milk teeth and the first molars just emerging.

The Taung baby – 'my baby', Dart calls it with feeling, perhaps revealing an absence that fate has left in his life. Dart was 32 years old at the time of the discovery; he had no doubt that his Taung baby represented an early ancestor of man and said as much boldly in his first reports on the fossil, which were prepared, he has said, 'proudly, and with a sense of history'.

The specimen represented a creature that was advanced beyond the apes in two distinctly human characteristics, its teeth and the 'improved quality' of its brain, Dart said. Furthermore, the forward position of the foramen magnum (the hole in the base of the skull through which the spinal cord passes) indicated that the Taung skull must have balanced on the top of the vertebral column in a manner similar to that of modern man. Therefore the creature had walked upright, he concluded, with hands free to become manipulative organs available for offence and defence. This proposal was rendered all the more probable, Dart reasoned, by the absence of 'massive canines and hideous features' in the specimen. The Taung baby represented the 'penultimate phase of human evolution', he wrote.

The press and the public loved it, but the scientific establishment was not impressed with either the fossil or the bold claims that this young man from South Africa was making for it. The Taung baby, or *Australopithecus* as it was officially known, was just another ape, they said and, in a manner of speaking, turned back to Piltdown and other larger-brained fossils then being dug from deposits in China – Peking Man.

The trouble with *Australopithecus* was not just the size of its brain, but also that it had been found in Africa. Most authorities inclined to the view that the Far East had been the site of man's origin. Java and Peking were near enough, so in fact was Europe (a lower jaw, dubbed Heidelberg Man, was found there in 1907), but Africa was way off the track, they believed.

Dart might have countered with more fossils, which doubtless were there to be found at Taung and other quarries. Adult and more complete specimens would have brought more substance to the argument and might even have settled it one way or the other. But instead he retreated from the controversy and applied his talents to the medical school.

Thereafter *Australopithecus* became little more than a music hall joke for the world at large, while in two or three hundred pages of highly technical description the scientists dismissed the claims of human ancestry and aligned the specimen with either the chimpanzee or the gorilla. And that might have been that, but for Robert Broom, who in May 1936 decided to go and have a look for 'an adult Taung ape'.

By then Robert Broom, 'scientific son of Richard Owen', was 69 years old. He already considered himself the greatest paleontologist that had ever lived and saw no reason why he should not now become the greatest anthropologist as well. But Broom was short of funds and could not afford to travel to Taung, so he began his search at a limestone quarry of similar antiquity at Sterkfontein, near Krugersdorp in the Transvaal, and within three months he found even more than he was looking for: an adult *Australopithecus* skull along with a complete endocranial cast. Broom dashed off a paper or two on the skull's relationship to the Taung specimen and its missing link status and kept on digging. The prizes came slowly, but by 1948, when Broom was 81 years old, he had assembled enough fossil teeth, jaws, skulls and skeletal remains to convince most people that *Australopithecus* had existed in gracile (slender) and robust form, had possessed teeth more man-like than ape-like, had walked upright and was a good candidate for the ancestry of man – just as Dart had said.

One might have thought that Broom's work would have left *Australopithecus* standing firmly on the evolutionary path that led to man. But the man-like jaw and the small ape-like brain (the exact opposite of the Piltdown evidence) did not satisfy everyone. Some still felt that a larger brain must have led the way. Whether this was due to residual effects of what might be called the Piltdown syndrome, or whether it stemmed from convictions of the kind that Richard Owen had expressed is impossible to tell, but the fact remains that although the *Australopithecus* brain was large for an ape, it was not large enough for all students of human evolution. And among the dissenters was a man who, along with his family, was destined to make some very important contributions to the study of fossil man: Louis Leakey.

Louis Leakey, born in 1903 to a missionary family settled in Kenya, found his first stone tool at the age of 12. From then on his life became a determined search for the origins of man – but he was not without his preconceptions. Leakey was educated in England while Piltdown still reigned; when he graduated from Cambridge in 1926 with first class honours in anthropology and archaeology, he held the firm belief that enlargement of the brain was a very early feature of man's evolution. He was also convinced that the ability to make stone tools was a crucial development.

The human brain is by far the most complex and highly organized structure on Earth. On average it weighs only 1,400 grams, but each cubic centimetre contains some six million cell bodies (called neurons), each of which is connected to as many as 80,000 other neurons. Although the brain itself is too soft to be fossilized, casts of the interior of fossil skulls (called endocranial casts) often show the exterior form of the brain in remarkable detail – in some cases even tiny blood vessels and nerves are visible. Endocranial casts provide important clues to the evolution of the brain.

This bas-relief is composed of restored endocranial casts of modern man (top right) and his primate ancestors. The basic structure of the brain is visible in the brain of the primitive insectivore *Ictops* (extreme left): at the front are the two olfactory bulbs, which deal with the sense of smell; behind them are the two bulges of the cerebrum where other sensory information is processed; and at the rear is the combined mass of the brainstem and the cerebellum, which control reflexes such as heart beat and respiration.

Two lines of brain evolution are shown diverging from *Ictops*. In the top row the tarsiiformes *Tetonius*, *Necrolemur* and *Rooneyia* show reduction in the size of the olfactory bulbs, and expansion of the cerebrum. In the lemuriformes the lower row, *Smilodectes* (two specimens), *Notharctus* and *Adapis* show similar development, with the cerebrum beginning to envelop the hind structure of the brain.

The cerebrum shows further expansion in the early apes (central group of three), *Aegyptopithecus* (two specimens) and *Proconsul*, and acquires even larger proportions in the hominids *Australopithecus boisei* (third from right) and *Homo erectus* (second from right), where the olfactory bulbs are concealed.

In *Homo sapiens*, modern man (top right), the cerebrum occupies 80 per cent of the total brain volume and with the many folds and convolutions of its surface, called the cerebral cortex, an enormous surface area of 2,500 square centimetres fits comfortably within the confines of the skull.

Leakey believed that man had been shaped several million years ago and had remained unchanged ever since. *Australopithecus* and the fossil specimens from Java, Peking and the Neander Valley were all evolutionary experiments which had ended in extinction, he said. They may have existed at the same time as the ancestors of modern man, but only as quite separate lineages without any direct connections. Archaeological evidence comprised a fundamental part of Leakey's anthropological beliefs. Only the ancestor of man had made stone tools, he said. And since no stone tools had ever been found that could be indisputably associated with the remains of *Australopithecus* found by Dart and Broom, the small-brained hominid was still further dismissed from the ancestry of man, in Leakey's view.

The Leakey name is most famously associated with the Olduvai Gorge in Tanzania. Louis Leakey first visited Olduvai in 1931, and soon realized that he had lit upon an anthropological and archaeological treasure house. It is an ancient lake basin dissected by a gorge up to 100 metres deep and the deposits exposed along the gorge walls cover a timespan of 1.9 million years, from the early Pleistocene to the Holocene (recent) epoch which began around 10,000 years ago. Where the gorge cuts through the ancient lake shorelines early hominid camp sites are exposed in all the ascending levels of the sequence, thereby providing a unique opportunity to trace hominid development over a known period of time. The camp sites are littered with stone tools, and with the remains of animals eaten there. Leakey could not have found a better place to look for the proof of his idea that a large-brained tool-making ancestor of man had existed in the early Pleistocene, along with or before the australopithecines, but in no way descended from them. The tools were there; all Leakey needed now were the remains of a large-brained hominid.

On his first visit to the gorge Leakey found stone tools within minutes of beginning to search. On subsequent visits, and throughout the intensive explorations that began in 1935, he and his companions collected hundreds more from all levels, but of the men who had fashioned them there was almost no evidence at all. While cratefuls of stone tools and mammalian fossils were gathered and written up, the hominid collection remained frustratingly small – two tiny skull fragments found in 1935, two teeth found in 1955 and another tooth found in 1959. That was all. For 30 years Leakey's theory remained just that – a theory without enough evidence to either prove or disprove its premise. And then, on 17 July 1959, Louis' wife Mary found a skull jutting from an early Pleistocene deposit.

The circumstances were remarkably similar to those surrounding the discovery of *Proconsul* at Rusinga Island in 1948. Louis was confined to his bed with influenza; Mary was taking the dogs for a walk when a piece of bone protruding from the ground caught her eye. Brushing aside a little soil, she uncovered teeth which, though very large, were definitely hominid. She rushed back to the camp shouting: 'I've got him! I've got him! I've got our man.'

Louis leapt from his bed and rushed to the site with Mary, but he did not share his wife's excitement for long. 'When he saw the teeth he was disappointed,' she says, 'since he had hoped the skull would be *Homo* and not *Australopithecus*.'

There cannot have been many occasions when evidence confounded preconception quite so dramatically. The discovery was tremendously important; the skull that the Leakeys had unearthed lay on the floor of a camp site, which was strewn with stone tools and split bones – presumably the remains of animals that the occupants of the site had eaten. This was the first time that hominid remains had been found indisputably associated with stone tools in early Pleistocene deposits. By any standard it could fairly have been said that the skull had belonged to the toolmaker and was therefore the oldest known ancestor of toolmaking man. The only trouble was that the skull was most definitely that of a small-brained *Australopithecus* and therefore a direct contradiction of Louis Leakey's views on the form of the human ancestor during the Pleistocene.

Most authorities would have been content to say that the discovery proved that *Australopithecus* had made tools after all and was therefore a better candidate for the ancestry of man than before. But Louis Leakey presented a somewhat different view when he published his announcement of the discovery.

Since the skull was found in association with tools he acknowledged that its owner must have been a toolmaker and concluded that the skull must represent the world's oldest man, but because he did not believe that *Australopithecus* was ancestral to man he gave the skull a different name – *Zinjanthropus boisei* – and assembled a list of 20 minor anatomical features which, he claimed, merited the specimen's generic distinction from *Australopithecus*.

While the overall significance of the discovery was acknowledged everywhere, Leakey's interpretations and the creation of a new genus were severely criticized in academic circles. However, the press and public welcomed *Zinjanthropus* unreservedly (his arrival coincided with the centenary of Darwin's publication of *The Origin of Species*), which doubtless helped Louis Leakey to assimilate both the academic criticism and the unsightly dent that *Zinj* made in his scheme of mankind's large-brained antiquity. How ironic then that not many months later, perhaps just as Leakey was adjusting to the idea that *Australopithecus* (alias *Zinjanthropus*) had made tools and was ancestral to man after all, the excavations funded by his energetic publicity campaign should turn up a specimen which dismissed *Zinj* from that exalted status. The fossils comprised some skull fragments, a lower jaw and some hand bones and, like *Zinj*, were found alongside stone tools, but they came from slightly older deposits, were more lightly built and indicative of a relatively large brain. Though fragmentary, the find came close to the very thing that Leakey had been hoping to discover for more than 30 years.

Leakey discreetly abandoned *Zinj* to his australopithecine affinities and today the specimen is formally called '*Australopithecus (Zinjanthropus boisei)*'. He named the new specimen *Homo habilis* (handy man) and told the world that here was the 'earliest man yet known to science' (dating from 1.9 million years ago). The discovery would revolutionize man's knowledge of his origins, he claimed, because it proved that two hominids had existed contemporaneously in the early Pleistocene, while most authorities had previously believed that man had evolved along a single line via *Australopithecus*.

Homo habilis was another great success in the public arena, especially when Leakey agreed in an interview that the child (the fossils were of a juvenile) could have died from a blow on the head and therefore might represent the world's first known case of murder. But again the fossils were not complete enough to convince all the academics that the Leakey theory of man's ancestry was now proven fact. Many scientists thought that the new specimen was very much like the gracile australopithecines and should be assigned to that genus, and even the anatomist who co-authored the original description of the new species once confessed that the association of stone tools was the most convincing evidence of its *Homo* status.

Nevertheless, *Homo habilis* survived the controversy. Indeed his status was even enhanced when a large-brained hominid skull was found in 1972 in Pleistocene deposits at East Turkana in northern Kenya and assigned to the same species. Popularly known as 1470 (its museum accession number), the skull was discovered by an expedition under the direction of Louis' son, Richard, just a few months before Louis died. It reunited father and son after many years of disenchantment and showed that in science, as in many things, there never was very much separating them. Like his father, Richard Leakey believes that human evolution has been a lengthy affair in which *Australopithecus* played no part. Predictably, 1470 was presented to the public as the world's oldest man and brought its promoter a taste of fame.

Subsequently, Richard Leakey's expeditions have retrieved a substantial collection of hominid fossils from the Turkana deposits. According to Leakey, this evidence now proves that *Homo* and *Australopithecus* existed at the same time – therefore *Australopithecus* cannot have been ancestral to modern man, he claims.

At around the same time, however, joint American and French expeditions to the Afar Depression in Ethiopia were also uncovering large quantities of hominid fossils. Their discoveries included skull and skeletal remains representing between 35 and 65 men, women and children, and a remarkable half-skeleton of a female hominid, now affectionately known as Lucy because the Beatles' song 'Lucy in the sky with diamonds' happened to be playing on the tape recorder when the first fragments of her skeleton were found protruding from a dry and dusty hillside.

The Afar hominids date from between three and four million years ago (the exact age is uncertain). None was more than 125 centimetres tall and each individual must have weighed between 25 and 50 kilograms; slight figures indeed in the ancient landscape, although adult males, it appears, may have been between 50 and 100 per cent larger than adult females. The fossils suggest that the brain was about the size of an ape's brain, the hands were capable of a powerful grasp and the hip, knee and ankle joints of Lucy and her companions leave no doubt that they walked with the habitual striding bipedal gait of modern man.

In one of the bold academic moves that distinguish their science, the leader of the Afar expeditions, Donald Johanson, and his co-authors have assigned their hominid discoveries to a single new species – *Australopithecus afarensis* – which, they claim, is ancestral to all other forms of early man. This claim conflicts mightily with the Leakey scheme of things, of course, and provoked considerable displeasure from that quarter, especially when Johanson and his team included as type specimen of their new species a fossil lower jaw that Mary Leakey had found at Laetoli, near Olduvai Gorge, in 1974.

Whether or not Johanson and his colleagues were justified in grouping the Laetoli jaw and the Afar fossils together when they were separated by over 1,600 kilometres in distance and half a million years in age, whether *afarensis* is a valid species, and whether it could have been ancestral to all hominids or only to the australopithecines, remains the subject of discussion and even, on occasion, surprisingly acrimonious argument among the experts. The intensity of feeling generated is probably directly related to the fact that for the time being, even though the Afar and Turkana collections provide a lot of detail, they leave the broad picture of man in the transition from ancestral ape to human tantalizingly incomplete.

Paradoxically, the picture seems much more complete at Laetoli, where Mary Leakey's teams have found very few fossil remains of early man, but have uncovered a haunting image of his presence there: a trail of footprints, fossilized in a patch of hardening mud that three individuals walked across 3.6 million years ago.

*   *   *

By all accounts the Laetoli landscape on the south-western edge of the Serengeti plain is not very different today from that which existed over three million years ago. Sadiman and Lemgarut are no longer active volcanoes, but they still stand high above the plain against the backdrop of the Ngorongoro highlands, their foothills covered in dense woodland, their upper slopes clothed in grass that turns from green to golden as the dry season advances.

From the volcanoes the plain stretches to a distant western horizon, a vast expanse of grassland broken here and there by the abrupt rise of hills at Naibardad, Naabi and Moru. In the shallow valleys strands of woodland mark the watercourses along which the seasonal rains drain away to the Olduvai Gorge, about 40 kilometres from Laetoli. Elephants come down to the plain from the highlands, tossing their heads as they catch the scent of a rhinoceros lurking in the thorn scrub;

giraffes cross the plain, their legs blurred in the shimmering heat haze; herds of zebra and antelope come here to graze; flocks of guinea fowl settle to feed; lions lie concealed in the dun-coloured grass. Laetoli preserves a precious sense of the Earth in its pristine state, when man was still wholly a part of nature.

Mary Leakey was attracted to the site by the discovery of some hominid fossils there during the course of a Christmas holiday visit in 1974. Expeditions in 1975 and 1976 found little more in the way of hominid fossil remains, but did discover much else of interest. Fossilized in the soft ashes with which the volcanoes had frequently dusted the landscape between about 3.59 and 3.77 million years ago were tiny leaves identical to those of the acacias that comprise the woodland today, mammals ranging in size from shrew to elephant, rodents, monkeys, tortoises and a clutch of beautifully preserved eggs matching those of the modern guinea fowl. Then one evening in September 1976, while returning to the camp in playful mood, Dr Andrew Hill, paleontologist, tripped and fell while trying to avoid a ball of elephant dung flung at him by Dr David Western, ecologist. At the time, they were crossing a small dry river bed in which a flat bare surface of hardened volcanic tuff was exposed. Expedition workers had passed that way dozens of times during the previous two seasons, but on this occasion the evidence that elephants used the route as well brought a new angle to the paleontologist's eye. While on his knees Andrew Hill noticed a curious spattering of tiny indentations in the flat grey surface. These were later identified as raindrop prints but, having attracted his attention, they led Dr Hill to examine the surface very closely. Among a profusion of puzzling indentations he found a quite unmistakable series of animal tracks.

Dr Hill's fortuitous fall changed the entire character of the Laetoli expeditions. Virtually overnight fossils were relegated to a league of secondary interest and during the final weeks of the 1976 season footprints of birds and mammals ranging from elephant and rhinoceros to cat and hare were found. In 1977 and 1978 seven sites were discovered. Mammal and bird prints occurred everywhere, wonderfully preserved in the ancient mud surfaces by the fine-grained dusts that had erupted from Sadiman, but most magical of all was the long trail of three hominids walking northward from the woodlands down to the plains.

Such conclusive evidence of function, older than any fossil hominid, leaves no doubt that man-like creatures walked this way 3.6 million years ago. The fossils from the Afar and from Laetoli itself suggest that the walkers had probably belonged to the *Australopithecus* lineage, with an ape-like skull containing a relatively small brain. What made them stand up and leave the forests that had nurtured the ancestral primates?

The ability to stand upright and scan long distances would have been a useful introduction to the expanding grasslands of the Miocene as the forests shrank and the arboreal niche became more crowded. And moving away from the trees, the pioneers probably ranged the

The small family group may seem to be a comparatively modern phenomenon, but some authorities believe that it was the predominant form of social organization among the human ancestors that roamed the African plains more than three million years ago.

savannas in small nomadic bands. Their upright stance would have freed their hands to gather food and carry things: they wielded sticks, perhaps, to dig up roots, knock down fruits or chase carnivores from their prey. The brain was small, but it was big enough to supplement the meagre physical attributes that carried the ancestral hominids from the forest.

No recognizably fashioned tools have been found at Laetoli or Afar, but this does not mean that the hominids of the day had not already crossed the first threshold of reason and were unable to identify problems and the means of solving them. They were probably using sticks and stones and other items quite habitually as the casually acquired implements of everyday life, and such things are not likely to have been preserved as recognizable tools. For more than one and a half million years after the three individuals walked across the mud at Laetoli, a unique combination of biological inheritance and environmental circumstance was enough to ensure the survival of their small, upright and lightly built kind. During that time they ranged down the length of Africa, establishing ancestral populations whose remains have subsequently been discovered in South Africa and Ethiopia, as well as in Tanzania and Kenya. And they were successful enough to diversify into at least two distinct species between about two and a half and two million years ago.

Along with the small and lightly built ancestral line, the larger and very heavily built specimens of *Australopithecus* appear in the fossil record around two million years ago, with massive jaws and molar teeth suggesting that they had moved away from the omnivorous lifestyle and were adapted to a predominantly herbivorous diet which required a lot of chewing. Leakey's *Australopithecus boisei* from Olduvai is an example of these robust australopithecines that were discovered and first described by Robert Broom in South Africa in the 1940s. During the 1970s they were found at East Turkana as well.

The robust australopithecines seem to have existed alongside their more gracile cousins successfully enough for a million years or more, but then they disappear from the fossil record without trace. Extinction is presumed to have been their fate, though why they should have become extinct remains a matter of debate. Their disappearance roughly coincides with the proliferation of *Homo habilis* and stone tool manufacture. It has been suggested that the robust herbivores were in fact wiped out by the gracile omnivores and their stone tools; this is a possibility, but in the absence of firm evidence it should be viewed as the kind of speculation to which the study of fossil man is all too prone.

Stone tools are the most evocative relics of our ancestors. Fossil bones may reveal the physical characteristics – height, weight, relative proportions of the body – but tools add an unexpected dimension of understanding. They may have lain undisturbed for nearly two million years, but we can be certain that the hand that made them all that time ago differed hardly at all from the hand that picks them up today. We heft them, think about using them and perhaps even imagine our lives depending upon them – which they do, in a sense. Our very existence is due to the success of the lifestyle adopted by our toolmaking ancestors. The cutting edge was the beginning of culture and technology. The crude stone tools found today are a tangible link with those beginnings.

The earliest stone tools generally recognized as such come from deposits at Olduvai Gorge that are about 1.9 million years old. They are simple, crude, chopping or mashing tools, generally made from oblong, smooth, water-worn cobbles that fit comfortably in the hand. The cutting edge was formed by knocking flakes alternately from either side at one end of the cobble. The observation that removing flakes from a stone may produce a useful sharp edge was almost certainly the result of natural accident. Rocks tumbling in a river or a landslide occasionally break, but such accidents are more rare than might be supposed, and the edge formed by accident is entirely unpredictable. So the really useful cutting edge must have been a rare treasure until someone perceived the benefits of a dependable supply and set about learning how the result of natural accident could be reproduced artificially.

Deliberately turning a stone into any kind of usable tool requires a lot of skill. Even with our present high level of general knowledge concerning technical matters, very few people today could decide which stone is best suited to the purpose and precisely where and how it should be struck to achieve the desired result. And we know it can be done – an incentive the first toolmakers lacked entirely. They had no examples to work from, but acquired their skills in pursuit of an end, driven by a need, served by the expanding potential of the hominid brain.

The advent of *Homo habilis* and stone tool manufacture coincides with the first evidence that the early hominids might have established occasional home bases in their cycle of nomadic wanderings. On the floor of Olduvai Gorge, at the level dated at 1.9 million years old, the Leakey excavations uncovered a circle of stones roughly four metres in diameter. At first sight the circle is not impressive, little more than a ring of loosely piled rocks, about 30 centimetres high, with six distinct heaps spaced along the northern rim where it is best preserved, but this is thought to be the very first evidence on Earth of a man-made structure. It is difficult to believe that the rock piles could have accumulated naturally; what is more likely is that they were put there, probably to support sticks that formed the frame of a windbreak – or even a hide.

Fossil fish and flamingo bones found at the site indicate a lakeside location, and fossilized rhizomes suggest that reeds or papyrus once grew there. The circle stands on a small hummock; it is not unreasonable to imagine that the spot was chosen because it was conveniently close to the lake and the creatures congregating there, but drier than the surrounding land. Concealed, lying quietly in wait, the hominids may well have trapped animals and birds from such a place.

Certainly the evidence suggests that meat became a more significant part of the diet around this time. Home-base sites are littered with

Modern man has existed for a mere 40,000 years – a minute fraction of the 3.5 billion years that life has existed on Earth, but time enough for the technology that began with the stone tool to have developed awesome consequence.

animal bones, many of them deliberately broken to extract the marrow, it seems. Stone tools became progressively more sophisticated, often made of specially selected materials brought from some distance away, and all apparently designed to speed up the butchering of animals. But meat in regular supply must be caught and killed (or stolen from predators), not simply gathered like plant food, so the changing diet would also have called for more cerebral software: more awareness of the surroundings, more reasoning power, more cunning – in short, a larger brain.

The brain of *Homo habilis* was indeed significantly larger than that of both the gracile and the robust australopithecines, and this in turn must have enhanced its own further development and called for a particular form of social organization.

The infants of large-brained adults must be born before their heads are too big to pass through the birth canal, even though they are hardly ready for it by that time, and early birth demands an extended period of parental care after birth. In theory, a secure home base and the division of labour between male and female along modern lines might thus have made some sense already at the *habilis* stage of human evolution. It is quite possible that the females stayed close to home with the children, gathering plant food perhaps, while the males went off hunting and brought back meat.

But this is only theory, stemming principally from the precepts of modern social systems and deriving very little from any hard evidence of the circumstances that confronted the human ancestors nearly two million years ago. From this distance in time, insulated by cities and civilization, we tend to forget that they were a part of the pristine landscape; potentially more significant, maybe, but at the time no more or less important, in terms of their physique or numbers, than a tree or an antelope.

The continuing search for hard evidence will eventually reveal more, it may even convert theory into fact, but for the time being all that can be said with certainty is that having walked away from the forest and picked up a stone, the upstanding and relatively large-brained primate was destined to become a rather special part of nature.

ACKNOWLEDGEMENTS

AUTHOR'S ACKNOWLEDGEMENTS

Photographs by John Reader

The photographs illustrating the opening of each chapter were taken specially for the book, incorporating original specimens, manuscripts, artifacts and pictures appropriate to the subjects. I am indebted to the institutions that permitted me to work on their premises, and to the individuals who helped me assemble the items I needed. Their co-operation, advice and kind assistance are very much appreciated.

Mr F.R. Maddison, Dr G.L'E. Turner, Mr A.V. Simcock and Mr J.G. Simons of the Museum of the History of Science, Oxford, facilitated the photograph for chapter 1 on page 14.

Barry Foster of the Geology Department, Imperial College, London; Sinclair Stammers, Burgess Daring Advertising and Chris Lovell provided the items I needed for the photograph in chapter 2, page 28.

The photographs for chapter 3 on page 42, and for chapter 5 on page 86, were taken at the British Museum (Natural History), with the co-operation, advice and help of Dr H.W. Ball, Dr Alan Charig, Dr Peter Forey and Sue Goodman.

The photographs for chapter 4 on page 66, chapter 6 on page 112 and chapter 8 on page 156 were taken at the University Museum, Oxford, courtesy of Dr W.J. Kennedy and with the assistance of Mr H.P. Powell. The portrait of Edward Lhywd incorporated in the photograph used in chapter 4 was kindly made available by the Librarian of the Ashmolean Museum, Oxford. Dr Schuyler Jones kindly provided a Danish flint dagger from the Pitt Rivers Museum, Oxford, for the photograph used in chapter 8.

The photograph for chapter 7 on page 128 was taken at the Charles Darwin Museum, Downe, courtesy of the Royal College of Surgeons and with the co-operation of Mr Philip Titheradge. The photograph features two of Darwin's notebooks from the *Beagle* voyage and paintings by John Gould from *The Natural History of the Voyage of the Beagle*. The magnolia was kindly supplied by Monique Regester.

Text

My principal aim in writing this book has been to tell a story – I have tried to bring together the facts of evolution and facts from the history of science in a continuous narrative that will tell an interesting and accurate story of both life on Earth and man's attempts to understand it. If I have succeeded, all well and good, but every reader should note that the pursuit of narrative inevitably imposes editorial constraints. I have not always given comprehensive accounts of contemporary discussion (and argument) on all the many points still under dispute. The reason for this is that such comprehensive coverage in an introductory book of this kind usually guarantees an incomprehensible text. So there is a good deal I have left out, and to maintain unity between the two threads of the story – evolution and science – I have adopted a rather traditionalist view of things that those at the cutting edge of science might regard as rather old-fashioned. Even so, I believe my position is defensible. I sought to pursue a comprehensible storyline through a fascinating subject. The interest the subject aroused in me was my principal guide, but my editorial decisions were never arbitrary nor matters of mere convenience. Indeed, having written this book, I would now urge interested readers to regard it as a starting point from which to explore and unravel the greater depth, breadth and fascination of the subject.

In my own explorations I have been heavily dependent upon the publications of many experts, and while I take full responsibility for any errors that may have crept in, the book could not have been written without their prior work, which I am pleased to acknowledge.

I am especially grateful for the time that Alan Charig, Peter Forey and Paul Whalley gave to my enquiries at the British Museum (Natural History), and it is a pleasure to acknowledge the courteous assistance I received from the staff of the following libraries:

The London Library
The General and the Paleontology Libraries of the British Museum (Natural History), South Kensington, London
The Royal Geographical Society Library

For general coverage of the subject the following titles are recommended, especially Helena Curtis's *Biology*, which is an outstanding and very readable book.

Attenborough D., 1979 London
Life on Earth

Bodenheimer F.S., 1958 London
The History of Biology: An Introduction

Curtis H., 1983 New York
Biology, 4th edition

Dawkins R., 1976 Oxford
The Selfish Gene

Gribben, J., 1981 London
Genesis

Halstead L.B., 1982 London
The Search for the Past

Laporte L.F. (ed.), 1982 San Francisco
The Fossil Record and Evolution: Readings from Scientific American

Lewin R., 1983 Washington DC
Thread of Life

Romer A.S., 1966 Chicago
Vertebrate Paleontology, 3rd edition

Romer A.S., 1968 New York & London
The Procession of Life

Taylor G.R., 1983 London
The Great Evolution Mystery

Wilson E.O., 1975 Cambridge Mass. & London
Sociobiology: The New Synthesis

In addition to the above, principal sources for each chapter were:

Chapter 1 (pp 14–27)

Bernal J.D., 1973 London
The Origin of Life

Day W., 1984 New Haven & London
Genesis on Planet Earth, 2nd Edition

Oparin, A.I., 1938 London
The Origin of Life

Chapter 2 (pp 28–41)

Cloud P., 1984
The Biosphere
(*Scientific American* 249: 132–144)

Margulis L., 1971
Symbiosis and Evolution
(*Scientific American* 225: 48–57)

Margulis L., 1981 San Francisco
Symbiosis in Cell Evolution: Life and its Environment on the Early Earth

Vidal G., 1984
The Oldest Eukaryotic Cells
(*Scientific American* 249: 32–41)

Chapter 3 (pp 42–65)

Agassiz E.C. (ed.), 1885 London
Louis Agassiz, Life and Letters

Lurie E., 1960 London
Louis Agassiz, A Life in Science

Romer A.S., 1968 Chicago & London
Notes and Comments on Vertebrate Paleontology

Weihaupt J.G., 1979 London
Explorations of the Oceans

Chapter 4 (pp 66–85)

Andrews H.N., 1980 London
The Fossil Hunters in Search of Ancient Plants

Chaloner W.G. & MacDonald P., 1980 HMSO London
Plants Invade the Land

Dunning F.W., 1981 HMSO London
The Story of the Earth

Dunning F.W. et al, 1978 HMSO London
Britain Before Man

Gass I.G. (ed.), 1972 London
Understanding the Earth

Gunther R.T., 1945 Oxford
Early Science in Oxford, vol. 14: *Life and Letters of Edward Lhwyd*

Morel P. & Irving R., 1978 London
Tentative Paleocontinental Maps for the Early Phanerozoic and Proterozoic
Journal of Geology 86: 535–61

Seward A.C. 1931 London
Plant Life through the Ages

Thackray J., 1980 HMSO London
The Age of the Earth

Thomas B., 1981 London
The Evolution of Plants and Flowers

Chapter 5 (pp 86–111)

Charig A., 1983 London
A New Look at the Dinosaurs

Colbert E.H., 1962 London
Dinosaurs, Their Discovery and Their World

Desmond A.J., 1982 London
Archetypes and Ancestors

Evans J., 1943 London
Time and Change: The Story of Arthur Evans

Halstead L.B. & J., 1981 London
Dinosaurs

Owen R., 1841 London
Report on British Fossil Reptiles
British Association for the Advancement of Science Report

Swinton W.E., 1970 London
The Dinosaurs

Chapter 6 (pp 112–127)

Charig A. & Horsfield B., 1975 London
Before the Ark

Desmond A.J., 1982 London
Archetypes and Ancestors

Findlay G., 1972 Cape Town
Dr Robert Broom FRS

Romer A.S., 1968 London
The Procession of Life

Chapter 7 (pp 128–155)

Desmond A.J., 1982 London
Archetypes and Ancestors

Halstead L.B., 1982 London
The Search for the Past

Huxley T.H., 1877 London
American Addresses

Ospovat D., 1981 Cambridge
The Development of Darwin's Theory

Owen R., 1849 London
On the Nature of Limbs

Owen R., 1868 London
Anatomy of Vertebrates, vol. 3

Romer A.S., 1968 London
The Procession of Life

Simpson G.G., 1951 London
Horses

Chapter 8 (pp 156-183)

Desmond A.J., 1982 London
Archetypes and Ancestors

Eiseley L., 1958 New York
Darwin's Century

Gruber H.E., 1974 London
Darwin on Man

Haeckel E., 1868 Berlin
Natürliche Schöpfungsgeschichte

Huxley T.H., 1863 London
Man's Place in Nature

Leakey M.L., 1984 London
Disclosing the Past

Ospovat D., 1981 Cambridge
The Development of Darwin's Theory

Owen R., 1849 London
On the Classification and Geographic Distribution of the Mammalia

Pilbeam D., 1984
The Descent of Hominoids and Hominids
(*Scientific American*, vol. 250: 84–96)

Reader J., 1981 London
Missing Links

Romer A.S., 1968 London
The Procession of Life

ARTIST'S ACKNOWLEDGEMENTS

All cultures have their own mythology about how they came about. It is my bias that our origins myth is an especially beautiful one, and perhaps the most imaginative of them all. We twentieth century humans find ourselves living in a time when there is growing evidence that our connection with nature is a profound one. We are part of a continuum that includes all life. Little by little we are unveiling a process that from simple organic molecules has produced thinking beings – ourselves – and indeed all living beings.

Historically, much of art has been about nature and our connection with it. Our understanding of the evolutionary process is now at a point where art can begin to explore this part of nature as well. I believe there are vast and exciting areas of this territory yet to be explored. Progress has been made in the writings of Loren Eiseley, the wonderful treatment by Stanley Kubrick in his film *2001*, and the photographs of John Reader. The latter led to our initial contact: standing in a bookstore in 1981, looking at the newly published *Missing Links*, I saw the fossils of our ancestors photographed for the first time in a way that captures their mystery and strikes the heart. It is a joy to work with someone who sees the fossils in this way.

Paintings and Illustrations

Sections of the *Tower of Time* (cover and pp. 41, 45, 47, 53, 58, 61, 76, 91, 101, 125, 153, 179, 182), The *Evolution of Horses* mural (pp. 145–9), and the *Transition to Land* mural (pp. 62–3) are reproduced courtesy of the National Museum of Natural History, Smithsonian Institution, where they are on display (© Smithsonian Institution 1980–1985). Special thanks go to Dr Richard S. Fiske and Robert A. Dierker for making this possible.

The *Archaeopteryx* painting on page 105 (© National Geographic Society 1982) is reproduced with the kind permission of the National Geographic Society.

For their generosity regarding copyright agreements I would also like to thank Smithsonian Books, Smithsonian Museum Shops and William Morrow and Co. Inc.

I would like to thank the following individuals for their scientific help, comments, support and assistance: Maurice Anderson, Sheryl Asherman, Li Bailey, Dr Robert T. Bakker, Eugene F. Behlen, Dr Anna K. Behrensmeyer, Dr Deb Bennett, Rachel C. Benton, Lesley Boone, William T. Boykins, Jr., Michael K. Brett-Surman, Professor Frank M. Carpenter, Jim Cherry, Chip Clark, Robert Augustus Closser III, Nancy J. Cocroft, Reginald B. Cocroft III, Spot Cocroft, Frederick J. Collier, Alan H. Cutler, Jim Dickerson, Dr William A. DiMichele, Dr Scott Z. Dolginow, Alexis Doster III, Elise Dreher, Dr Robert J. Emry, Dr Helen E. Fisher, Dr Peter M. Galton, Mr and Mrs Richard F. Gamble, Dr C. Lewis Gazin, Sir Thomas W. Gray, Carolyn C. Gurche, Charley P. Gurche, John C. Gurche, Suzanne T. Gurche, Dr Jessica

Harrison, Dr Leo Hickey, Dr Francis M. Hueber, Dr Ralph Holloway, Dr Nicholas Hotton III, Sally H. Love, Lynn McDonald, Dr Ian G. Macintyre, Dr Larry D. Martin, Elizabeth Miles, Richard Molinaroli, George Nicholas, Dr Storrs L. Olson, Laurence P. O'Reilly, Dr John H. Ostrum, Edward Owen, Gregory Paul, Dr Rick Potts, Robert W.Purdy, Dr Leonard B. Radinsky, Meridith Rinaldi, John M. Roberts, Dr J. William Schopf, Dr H.P. Schultze, David M. Seager, Sue Smith, Michael L. Tiffany, Catharine Valentour, Dr Scott L. Wing.

INDEX

Numbers in italic refer to captions and
illustrations.